As a meditator of 15+ y [new in this book. Overv] *roadblock to why peop... ....*
tionships and life. This incredibly practical guide
teaches specific tactics to use when your emotions get
out of control. Plenty of examples are given to illus-
trate how the techniques work, and a generous dose of
humor is thrown in to make this an enjoyable read. I
highly recommend reading Detlef Beeker's Master Your
Emotions!

John Weiler - Author of "An Ordinary Dude's Guide
to Meditation"

I really like the books of Prof. Beeker: easy to under-
stand, amusing to read and straight to the point. The
book "Master Your Emotions" is packed to the brim
with effective techniques. The new approach of the
book makes negative emotions even easier to combat.

Som Bathla – Author of "The Intelligent Thinking"

Many people talk about emotional intelligence. But I
have found few emotion experts or psychologists who
actually know what it is, and even fewer who can teach
you how to obtain it. In his gem of a new book, Master
Your Emotions, psychologist, stress expert and happi-
ness researcher Dr. Detlef Beeker breaks new ground
by revealing a precise formula for helping you apply
some of the best available strategies for coping with
stressful emotions, based upon how intensely you may
be feeling them. In my estimation, this is a very im-

portant book which should be read and applied by anyone wishing to become happier, more productive, and more emotionally stress-free.

Dr. Mort Orman, M.D. – Author of "The 14 Day Stress Cure" and one of America's leading stress elimination experts

More books by Prof. Dr. Detlef Beeker

Stress is an Illusion

Stress is a Decision

The 90-Day Happiness Journal

Master Your Emotions

The New 5-Step System to End Anxiety, Defuse Anger and Defeat Depression & Negative Thinking

Prof. Dr. Detlef Beeker

www.detlefbeeker.de/en/

Prof. Dr. Detlef Beeker

Happiness Researcher

Master Your Emotions Copyright © 2019
by Prof. Dr. Detlef Beeker

ISBN 978-3-9821013-0-9

Disclaimer

Contents

Free Gift

Below is the link to my book **18 Surprising, Good-Mood Tips** (52 pages). Feel free to download it!

http://detlefbeeker.de/en/gift/

Do you remember the first time you fell in love? Wasn't everything suddenly wonderful? The blue sky looked so beautiful with its puffy, white clouds. You could even enjoy rain! What if you could have this lovely mood all the time?

In this book, you will learn:

- **Body parts** to press to relieve stress and im-

prove your mood and health
- Proven mental tactics that will put you in a **good mood in seconds**
- **Secret Yoga techniques** that will easily increase your good mood
- The **unknown piece of music** that is scientifically proven to be the best stress reducer
- What you can learn from **James Bond** and how it gives you relaxation and self-confidence
- How you can relax in **10 seconds**
- Practice this **mind-boggling technique** and to be refresher and revitalized
- The **best apps** to relieve your stress and give you relaxation and serenity
- The **Fidget Cube** and how it works
- Bonus: The **new generation** of good mood techniques
- ... and much more

Download this book **NOW for free** so that you'll be guaranteed more joy, serenity, and happiness with the help of the best techniques.

http://detlefbeeker.de/en/gift/

About the Author

"The universe is friendly."

International Amazon best-selling author Prof. **Dr. Detlef Beeker** is a happiness researcher and anti-stress expert. He has been researching these fields for more than 20 years and has written numerous books. Detlef is not just an author but also someone who practices what he writes. He has been meditating for more than 20 years.

Too many self-help guides give you big ideas but fail to show you how they are actually applicable. In his books, Detlef Beeker offers practical methods and step-by-step instructions that you can implement immediately.

At the age of 7, Dr. Beeker had already found his destiny. "I want to become a taster in a pudding factory," he told his mum. Although his vocation has changed since then, his deep desire to make the world a better place has remained.

Visit his website http://detlefbeeker.de/en to find lots of helpful tips, tricks, and a gift for you!

Introduction

"Our real purpose is to be happy."
– Dalai Lama

In this chapter...

- Why this book is different and even revolutionary
- Diversity of methods and the 5-step peace process
- How emotions arise — be prepared for a surprise
- Why the author has a talkative Darth Vader in his head and so do you!
- What are the exact starting points for controlling emotions?

The key to controlling emotions and why it has been overlooked

This book you're reading is different. It is revolutionary, if I may say so myself. It isn't a great revolution, like the American Revolution, but rather a small one, like the *Emder Revolution* in North Germany. But the book has a brand new approach that improves the effectiveness in dealing with emotions.

I have discovered a key factor in controlling emotions that has not yet been taken into account. It took me 20 long years to find this factor. Do you want to know what this key to controlling emotions is? Let's make a comparison:

If you have a slight cough, you take a light, herbal cough syrup. But once your cough has matured into full-grown pneumonia, you need to take strong antibiotics. That is, the intensity of your illness requires different remedies.

This is the same with emotions. A slight restlessness requires a different remedy than a panic attack. It makes sense, doesn't it? Surprisingly, this has not been done so far. The idea that the techniques should be adapted to the intensity of your feelings has not been systematically applied in any therapy or guidebook.

This is the novelty of this book. This is the revolutionary approach. For the first time, psychological-techniques are systematically assigned to different emotional intensities. As a result, the techniques are tailor-made and have a much better effect.

Let me give you an example:

If you are plagued by an unpleasant but slight restlessness, I recommend the technique "Expansion." It's an acceptance technique. If, on the other hand, you have full-blown panic attacks, I will prescribe a preventive technique, "The Work," and an acute technique, the powerful "Anti-Panic Breathing". You work preventively so that panic doesn't even occur. However, if it does occur, you can successfully use anti-panic breathing. It would be wrong to use the expansion technique in case of panic. Accepting panic, giving it space — that's almost impossible. Therefore: different intensities, different techniques.

You can look up which techniques you use in which situations in a table which I designed especially for you. It couldn't be simpler.

The key: Light emotions are fought with light techniques; strong emotions are fought with strong techniques. Logical, isn't it?

Furthermore, the book is characterized by a **variety of methods**. I have taken psycho-techniques from all kinds of therapies and approaches. My only criterion was: "How effective is this technique?" You will find in this book only the absolutely best techniques. All have proven their effectiveness in hundreds of thousands of people. By the way, a variety of methods cannot be taken for granted. Many approaches are limited to a few techniques.

In this book you'll discover...

- A brand new concept, which is crucial for you to control your emotions. This concept is based on the author's 20 years of experience and research.
- How emotion prophylaxis frees you from strong negative emotions.
- The surprising truth of how emotions are created.
- The **5-step peace process**, the simple recipe

for inner peace. It shows you step-by-step which techniques you apply and for how long.

- A simple technique that modern psychothera-pists and ancient Greek philosophers use to prevent negative feelings from arising in the first place.
- How to resolve stress, worries, and fears in seconds with a scientifically proven technique.
- Special, extremely powerful **Anti-Panic Breathing** with which you are guaranteed to get panic under control.
- Know the **new generation** of thought-stop techniques. This way you are guaranteed to stop your negative thoughts immediately.
- How the revolutionary **Sedona** method lets go of your negative emotions in seconds. This technique has proven itself a hundred thou-sand times over.
- How you use the paradoxical technique of de-fusion to trick your inner critic.
- Hardly-known power tactics and tricks against depression.
- How to turn your Angry Monster into a purr-ing kitten with two simple tricks.
- ... and much more.

My talkative Darth Vader

My Aunt Dorothea talked a lot. She was a bit chubby, and I only knew her with grey hair, which she wore as a perm. She looked like Miss Doubtfire. I remember when I was little — maybe eight or nine years old — I would sit down on our big brown sofa and lean back on it. She would talk about something or other — I think it was her neighbor. It was comfortable, and I fell asleep under the torrent of her words. After about half an hour, I woke up, and she was still talking. My Aunt Dorothea hadn't noticed that I had fallen asleep. I guess it wasn't very important to her if I was listening, she just wanted to talk.

My Aunt Dorothea reminds me of the voice in my head. It's also yakking away without a dot or a comma. We have about 80,000 thoughts a day. That is, every second, a new thought buzzes through our head. The unfortunate thing is, most of the thoughts we have are negative. The voice in our head insults us, degrades us, and frightens us. "You're not good enough!" is one of its favorite phrases. So we have a villain in our heads who is extraordinarily chatty.

Have I told you I'm a big Star Wars fan? The head villain is Darth Vader. The voice in my head is talkative like Aunt Dorothea and sometimes mean like Darth Vader. So I have a talkative Darth Vader in my head! My talkative Darth Vader is always criticizing me and telling me what's going to go wrong.

Life isn't easy with such a chatty Darth Vader. Surprisingly, we all have a voice in our heads that doesn't seem particularly well-disposed.

"It was at that moment, I was in bed at night, realizing for the first time that the voice in my head — the constant commentary that has dominated my consciousness since I can remember — was some kind of asshole."
– Dan Harris

I couldn't have said it better: the voice in our heads is some kind of asshole. This voice makes life difficult for us; she draws horror scenarios and announces what a failure we are. Here's the best part: the talkative Darth Vader means well. He doesn't want to hurt me. No, he wants to protect me. Let's take a closer look:

1. Negative feelings are important for survival:
Our brain isn't about us feeling good. No, we're supposed to survive. Our brain is a survival expert. Our ancestors were constantly struggling with dangers: hunger, wild animals, and accidents. Our ancestors could be attacked by a tiger at any time. Our brains had to be on guard. Every hint, however small, was checked to see if it posed a threat. Better to assess a harmless situation as dangerous than a dangerous situation as safe. Our brain is looking for danger — it used to be vital; today it is unnecessary. Our world is quite safe; we die of old age rather than of a tiger attack.

So that means my talkative Darth Vader is paranoid. He's always seeing threats that don't even exist. He doesn't mean any harm.

2. Emotions are signals: Fear tells us, for example, that something is threatening to go wrong in the future. We may have to make a speech, but we are not ideally prepared. So we should not just dismiss our negative feelings but also see if they can tell us something meaningful.

3. Feelings are always neutral: An interesting theory says that (negative) feelings are neutral. Only our labelling makes them unpleasant. Let's take an example of this argument:

Sebastian has to give a speech, and he's afraid. This manifests itself in an accelerated heartbeat and other body sensations. But since when is a faster heartbeat a bad thing? Fear is very similar in body sensations to the feeling of excitement. Sebastian adds the label "fear" to these body sensations. Someone else would probably interpret the same bodily sensations as excitement.

Why are there so many people who like skydiving or bungee jumping? Because for them, fear is a positive thing. It brings them to life! If we disregard the label "fear" above, the body sensations remain. Body sensations for themselves are not negative but neutral.

That argument is interesting. It helps to accept negative feelings. When negative feelings arise, we should focus on the body's sensations and not on the negative thoughts that go with them. Why? Because the body sensations themselves are not negative. The whole thing is perceived as negative and unpleasant only by the associated negative evaluations.

So, now I've taken up the cudgels for my talkative Darth Vader. He's not the bad guy everyone claims he is. Nevertheless, his constant negativity is annoying. And the good news is there's something we can do about it. How to control our talkative Darth Vader is what this book is about. We will learn to control our

18

emotions. The decisive starting point for this is that we tame the negative voice in our heads. Or at least not believe her.

The bad news

As you may know, I'm a professor. One topic I present in my lectures is happiness science. As the name suggests, it's all about being and becoming happy. A few semesters ago I was discussing this subject when a student said, "Mr. Beeker, I will be watching you from now on!" I asked, "Why? Do I have to be afraid?" He said, "If I catch you in a bad mood, I'll pass it on!"

This is a misunderstanding. No person in this world can always be happy and in a good mood. Not even the Dalai Lama. Always trying to be in a good mood is stressful. Russ Harris described this excellently in his famous book, He Who Follows Happines, Runs Past It. If we want to hold on to happiness, it escapes us. It's not always possible to be in a good mood. Life has its ups and downs. We can't control it. We will be in pain, we will get sick and even die. Other misfortunes will befall us. We're going to lose loved ones; maybe we're going to crash or we're going to lose our jobs. Unfortunately, life offers countless possibilities, which bring us into difficult situations.

Let us try to accept this. Let us accept that unpleasant feelings are part of life. That makes it a lot easier. Everyone has unpleasant feelings. Trying to be always in a good mood only leads to even more suffering. Harvard professor Tal Ben-Shahar described this as "the permission to be human." Allow yourself to be human. Let's not try to always be on top of things. It just makes unnecessary stress. If we're sad because a loved one died, that's natural. This feeling has a right to be there. If we now have the belief that we should always be in a good mood, it only makes us feel even worse. Sadness is now joined by self-reproaches.

Our society promotes this. Positive feelings can be expressed; negative feelings cannot. Society tells us, "You should be in a good mood!" If you're in a bad mood, there's something wrong with you. That's nonsense, of course. Let's not be influenced by this. We have a right to our negative feelings.

Nevertheless, it is possible to significantly reduce our suffering. The Dalai Lama is more content than an average person. He uses wise techniques and can thus meet many storms of life peacefully. In this book you will learn the best techniques so that you can go through life like the Dalai Lama.

The missing link: how emotions are created

Let's look at the way emotions are generated. By the way, I'm not making it unnecessarily complicated: I use the terms "feelings" and "emotions" synonymously. Back to the topic: How do emotions arise? I have to go back a bit. Most people assume that events trigger our feelings. I didn't get the job, so I'm disappointed. My boss criticized me, so I'm hurt and angry.

My friend cheated on me, so I'm hurt and mad. We can continue this list indefinitely. But is it really so? The clear answer is no! It's the thoughts we have about a certain event that trigger our emotions. Already 2000 years ago the former slave and great philosopher Epictetus recognized:

"It's not the things themselves that worry us, but the ideas and opinions about things."

Epictetus was born in 50 AD. He was a slave in Rome. Life as a slave was very uncertain; he constantly feared being beaten or even killed. Epictetus's master ordered that his leg smashed. Since then Epictetus limped. To be able to endure such a life was a challenge. Fortunately, Epictetus had access to the Stoic teachings when he was still a slave. Stoicism is a philosophical direction and is known for the fact that its philosophers are always calm. Thus Epictetus recognized that he could also be happy as a slave, since it was not the events themselves that made him suffer, but his beliefs and thoughts about it. Later Epictetus was released and founded his own school of philosophy. He is considered one of the greatest and most influential Stoics.

Is that good or bad? It's great! It means that we are

independent of external events. If you lose your job, you can still be happy. If your partner dumps you, you can still be satisfied. You just need to change your attitudes and thoughts. This is much easier than changing events. It's very difficult to get your partner to continue your relationship. Changing your attitude about it, on the other hand, is easy. This is the basis of cognitive behavioral therapy (CBT). It is a very effective form of therapy:

"Cognitive behavioral therapy is the most time- and cost- effective psychotherapy
for depression and anxiety."
– Dr. Andrew Weil

Negative thoughts trigger negative emotions. But that's not all. There is another link in the chain that is often ignored. It's the fusion. This means that we believe our negative thoughts and consider them important. The fusion is of central importance to the negative feelings developing. Because if we simply do not believe our thoughts, no negative feelings arise. So when I think, "I'm a failure," but I just don't believe it, then I'm unaffected — there's no negative feeling. The problem is, we can't turn off our thinking. We can slow down our thinking, for example in meditation, but our thinking will always be there. Thoughts come and go — like ebb and flow. So the crucial point is how do I deal with my negative thoughts?

The figure shows this causal chain:

- First we have the triggering situation. For example, our boss criticizes us.
- Now, our thoughts and attitudes come to this triggering situation. We think, "My boss is such an ass! I did everything right! Why is he criticizing me? He doesn't like me! That is so unfair! I'll never get anywhere around here." Such negative thoughts would lead to negative feelings if there were not another intermediate step.
- Fusion means we believe our minds. We believe our boss is unfairly criticizing us. We believe he's an ass. But we can also decide not to take these negative thoughts seriously. If we can do this, we call this defusion. Therefore, thoughts and feelings do not merge.
- The last step in the causal chain is emotion. We have negative thoughts, we believe them, and there is a feeling of anger or frustration.

In this process we can mainly work on the two middle building blocks. It is very difficult to control our external situation at all times. Unfortunately, we cannot prevent our boss from criticizing us, our partner from insulting us, or from becoming ill. But we can work on getting a better mindset on certain situations. We can replace our negative thoughts with true thoughts. The second possibility is that we defuse. So we allow negative thoughts, but we simply do not believe them. So we are starting with the third building block. All the techniques in this book are extremely effective and apply to either the second or third building block.

In a nutshell

- The revolutionary thing about this book is that different techniques are systematically assigned to different emotional intensities. This makes the techniques that are recommended to you tailor-made and very effective.
- In addition, the book has many other features, such as a variety of methods and the five-step peace process, which allow you to control emotions in particularly effective ways.
- The voice in our head makes life difficult for us. She talks all the time; we have about one thought per second. Unfortunately, most thoughts are negative.
- Negative thoughts only lead to negative emotions when we believe them. This is called a fusion.
- So to control our emotions, we can work on

24

our negative thoughts or we can work on not fusing.

My story: I was a hypochondriac

"99% of all the things you worry about will never happen!"
–- Anonymous

L aura!" I yelled in a shrill voice, "Hurry up, come here!"

My heart was beating, my palms were freezing cold. Laura turned the corner leisurely: "What is it?" She was my girlfriend at the time. Laura was tall and had long, brunette hair. Under her pony, funny, lively eyes sparkled.

"I have cancer," I gasped in a suffocated voice.

"Again," Laura replied unimpressed.

"Hey, what is this? It's true! You can feel my larynx here," I cawed outraged at her serenity in view of my approaching death. I was in my late 20s and hypochondriac. I was almost 2 m tall and had eaten a small belly out of frustration. At that time cancer was my main fear. I constantly felt my body whether there was a bump or a knob. On this morning I had palpated my larynx and felt a small increase. That had to be laryngeal cancer! I was firmly convinced of that.

Laura felt demotivated at my larynx: "I don't feel anything", she said and suppressed a yawn.

"Yes, yes! There's something I felt it clearly," I scribbled. In fact, there was a little swelling on my larynx.

"Then go to the doctor if you are unsure," Laura replied rationally.

I thought about it and came to the conclusion after an objective and careful analysis of the situation:
"No, no, afterwards the doctor discovers that I really have cancer. That would be terrible. No, I don't go to the doctor. I better wait."
Laura rolled her eyes: "Let's have breakfast, I'm starving."
"I can't eat now," I said dramatically.
"OK, see you soon," Laura fluted and walked out of the room.

If you think this episode was over, you're way off. I spent the next few months constantly palpating my larynx. Every time I did this, horror thoughts came to me: This is a tumor. It was bigger than yesterday, wasn't it? I will surely die soon. I should make my will. Many months I passed like this, I suffered and fear was my constant companion.

But then everything changed. It came unexpected as life is. I can still remember exactly that day today: it was autumn, the leaves had turned brown and yellow, but it was not cool. I was on my way to my favorite bookstore. It was a small shop stuffed with books. At the edge a small bar on which a cash register was trohnte and behind it the bookseller sat, like an oversized mole. He had tiny eyes and thick nickel glasses balanced on a small, pointed nose. I stepped into the shop, a bell sounded.
The bookseller didn't look up: "How are you, Detlef?"
"How do you know it's me," I replied in surprise: "I'm

not so well," I complained: "You know, that cancer."
"Yes, yes, just look around," the bookseller said un-impressed.
Indignant at his disinterest in my fate, I stepped up to the leaning shelf where the books on psychology and self-help were gathered. I have often stood in front of this shelf, but none of the books ever appealed to me. "Huh, is the book new?" I shouted to the bookseller. A new book caught my eye, *How To Stubbornly Refuse To Make Yourself Miserable About Anything-yes, Anything*, it was from Albert Ellis. I pulled the book off the shelf. I thought, *hmm, I feel miserable! That fits!* Curiously I opened the book. I began to read. "Interesting", I mumbled to myself. I continued read-ing, I couldn't stop, page after page I turned over. "The book seems to be good. The bookseller stood right next to me. I hadn't heard him coming.
Shocked, I spun around: "Yes, uh, hmm, yes," I stut-tered.
"You've been standing in front of this shelf for 2 hours now, reading the book," the bookseller said gently.
"Really? That's how long I've been standing here," I said in disbelief. The book had really fascinated me. It was about our thoughts and beliefs triggering our negative feelings and not what happens. So it wasn't this swelling, this little bump on my larynx that frightened me, but my thoughts about it. That was tremendous, it struck me like lightning. I bought the book and ran home. That evening I read the whole

book. It contained many exercises and reflections. Between us, I can be quite lazy sometimes, but I did all the exercises and tasks for this book. I quickly realized that I was pretty messed up and that my head was teeming with irrational thoughts and according to Albert Ellis irrational thoughts lead to negative feelings.

The book brought a turn in my life. I am very grateful to Albert Ellis for writing this book. It was not always easy to work with this book. Becoming aware of one's beliefs is often liberating, but can also be painful. Over the next few weeks I spent a lot of time on this book and made good progress. I gained more and more inner peace. After three weeks I was ready to announce Laura resolutely:
"Tomorrow I will make an appointment with the doctor."
Laura looked at me with big eyes: "Really? Super! I'm coming with you."
A few days later we went to the doctor together, I was nervous. To make a long story short, it wasn't cancer. I would have worried all these months unnecessarily.
I started reading other self-help books, no, devouring them. It was incredible, you could do something about your worries and fears. From that point on there was no stopping. I read, attended workshops, started meditating and finally I earned my crust with it. I discovered some very effective methods from which you will get to know a handful in this book.

If I hadn't had this fear of cancer many, many years ago, there wouldn't be this book you're reading right now. By the way, the technique of Albert Ellis has also been included in this book in a slightly improved version. You can find it in the chapter "How you control very intense emotions".

How to find the ideal technique for you

"Don't give up until you meet happier feelings."
– Chuck Spezzano

In this chapter...

- How much feelings influence you depends on their intensity and frequency
- The more intense the feelings, the stronger the techniques must be
- Find your customized techniques with the Emotions Matrix

The revolutionary Emotions Matrix

I assume you have an unpleasant feeling that you want to work on — maybe fear, worry or anger. Maybe you're suffering from depression or a lack of forgiveness. Do you have an emotion in mind that you would like to get rid of?

How disturbing a negative feeling is depends on two factors:

1. Intensity: How intense or strong is the feeling? Let's take the example of "fear." The intensity can be slightly intense. That means there is only a sense of restlessness. But the intensity can also be maximum, which would be panic. In this book we use a scale of 0-4. Zero means that there is no negative feeling at all. At four, the feeling is very intense.

0 = no negative feeling noticeable

1 = slightly intense, e.g. restlessness

2 = moderately intense, e.g. anxiety

3 = quite intense, e.g. clear fear

4 = very intense, e.g. panic

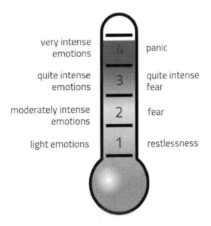

very intense emotions	4	panic
quite intense emotions	3	quite intense fear
moderately intense emotions	2	fear
light emotions	1	restlessness

The image shows the four intensity levels.

2. Frequency: This is the second important influencing factor. The more often an unpleasant feeling occurs, the more it affects our lives. The scale used in this book ranges from "rare" to "permanent."

rare = several times a week

occasionally = at least once a day

often = several times/frequently per day

permanent = several times per hour

However, these figures are only approximate values. What we find "rare" is ultimately subjective and also depends on the type of emotion. A panic attack is perceived as more disturbing, even if it only occurs once a week, than, for example, an outburst of anger. Therefore, the frequency information is only a guide. Ultimately, what counts is your subjective feeling. Nevertheless, I recommend that you first stick to the information; it has proven itself.

It is obvious that we choose other techniques depending on whether a feeling is light or very intense and how often it occurs. We need to take a different medicine if we have a mild chest cough than if we have pneumonia. Surprisingly, this has not yet been systematically taken into account in any therapy approach or other system. This book systematically assigns techniques to different frequencies and intensities for the first time.

In this book I have collected the best techniques so that you can control your emotions. The more your life is influenced by unpleasant feelings, the stronger the corresponding counter techniques must be. If you feel only a slight restlessness, you can work well with the "Expansion" technique, i. e, in the following table you will find the right techniques for your special situation. So you just have to consider how often this unpleasant feeling occurs and how intense it is. So ask yourself:

- How intense is the unpleasant feeling I want to get rid of? Classify this on a scale from 1 = slightly intense to 4 = very intensive. You can't do anything wrong. Rely on your gut and don't think too long. You can change your decision at any time.
- How often do I feel the negative feeling? You can decide whether you feel the emotion rarely (several times a week), occasionally (at least once a day), often (several times/frequently per day), or even constantly (several times an hour). The values in parentheses are for guidance only. It depends on how you feel.

Frequency Intensity	rare (several times a week)	occasionally (at least 1 x per day)	often (several times/frequently per day)	permanent (several times per hour)
1 = light	Expansion	Expansion	Expansion	Expansion
2 = moderate	Defusion/ 4-7-8 Breath	Defusion/ 4-7-8 Breath	Defusion/ 4-7-8 Breath	Defusion/ 4-7-8 Breath
3 = quite	Sedona/ Delete Button	Sedona/ Delete Button	Sedona/ Delete Button	TheWork
4 = very	Sedona/ Delete Button	TheWork	TheWork	TheWork

When you decide, check the Emotion Matrix.

Lisa worries a lot. When this occurs, the feeling is not strong. Lisa estimates the intensity to be a two. But the worries are there all the time. This means that the techniques that can be considered are "defusion" and "4-7-8 breath." These techniques didn't appeal to her. The Emotions Matrix is always just a suggestion; you don't have to stick to it slavishly. That's why I suggest-

ed the "Delete Button." The Delete Button Technique is particularly effective for worries. Lisa agreed with me that she would practice this technique for a week and see what happens. After one week the worries had already improved considerably. We agreed that Lisa would run the technique for a total of three weeks. After that, the whole story had improved so much that Lisa abandoned the technique. The worries came back here and there but could be accepted by Lisa.

The goal is that either the negative emotions no longer appear, or that we can accept them. This means that we no longer fight an emotion, but we can let it be there without reservations. It's not bothering us anymore, so we can give the emotion room. Acceptance is a very important concept. If we accept emotions, we are at peace with them. This means, for example, that we can be afraid and at the same time be at peace. The less we fight an emotion, the sooner we can let it go.

In a nutshell

- The Emotions Matrix shows you which techniques are perfect for you.
- For light emotions, the Expansion technique is the antidote.
- You can fight moderately intense feelings optimally with the 4-7-8 breath or the defusion.
- You can control quite intense emotions with the Sedona method or the Delete Button.

- You should fight very intense feelings preventively with The Work. In addition, choose another technique that is designed for acute situations.

The best techniques for light to very intense emotions

"A smooth sea does not make a skilled sailor."
– Anonymous

In this chapter…

- The techniques of this book are explained in detail
- Also explained are which techniques work best with emotions of varying intensity

The techniques are at the heart of this system. These are all handpicked premium techniques that are guaranteed to work. Why do I know that? Because these techniques have already helped hundreds of thousands of people.

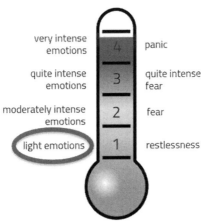

How to control light emotions

In this section, we deal with light emotions, such as "restlessness."

The "Expansion" technique is particularly suitable for getting a grip on unpleasant emotions. This technique comes from ACT (Acceptance and Commitment Therapy). It is a technique of acceptance. The term "expansion" indicates that we give room to the unpleasant feeling. So we are not defending ourselves against this feeling; on the contrary, we are giving it room. Accepting a feeling is a very important ability. The more negative feelings we can accept, the more we are at peace. That means the negative feeling is there, but it doesn't bother us.

How do we accept a negative feeling? The trick is that we don't listen to our talkative Darth Vader but instead pay attention to our body sensations. Why are we doing this? I need to do a little explanation on that. An emotion consists of two building blocks:

- The triggering and accompanying negative thoughts
- The corresponding body sensations

Let's look at an example:

Lara is worried about her child. Her child has a slight fever and cough. The talkative Darth Vader in her head whispers to her: "The fever will rise! She'll get pneumonia. Watch yourselves!" With such negative thoughts, it's no wonder Lara's worries are getting worse. She feels the worry as a weak feeling in her stomach, a restless sensation in the middle of her body, and sweaty palms.

This example is a good illustration of how negative emotions work. Negative thoughts trigger corresponding body sensations. These together make up the emotion. Lara has a weak feeling in her stomach etc. The negative thoughts go on, and as long as we hear them, we get involved in this story. That's why it's good to pay attention to our body sensations. Even if these are supposedly negative, they are simply body sensations. Our body is always in the here and now. Our thoughts are always somewhere else. Paying attention to our body grounds us and takes us away from this negative story that we tell ourselves.

We don't just pay attention to our body sensations; no, we go one step further. We give them room. With light feelings this is usually not difficult. A restlessness occurs, we give the feeling space, and that's it. Emotions that we really give a lot of space quickly disappear. If we fight them, however, they stay. The problem: our natural reaction is to fight the unpleasant. Acceptance or expansion is therefore something counter-intuitive. The more unpleasant the feeling, the harder it is for us to accept it. A slight restlessness is still ok, but we definitely want to get rid of a full-grown panic. That's why I recommend other techniques for more intense feelings.

Expansion

Goal: make peace with unpleasant feelings

Technique:

1. Observe without judging your physical sensations. If an unpleasant feeling, such as fear, rises, direct your attention to these physical sensations. Be as curious as a scientist. Examine your body sensations. Does it feel warm or cool? Where exactly does the body sensation occur? What color is it? Play around with it. It is important that you focus your attention on your body and not on your thoughts.

2. Breathe slowly and consciously into and around the feeling. As if you wanted to give it more room. A slow, deep abdominal breathing is always calming. It may not make your feeling disappear, but it is a peaceful anchor in the eye of the storm.

3. Allow the feeling to be there; give it space. Focus your attention on the physical sensations. That feeling may be unpleasant, but you let it be there. You're not fighting that feeling. You accept it. This can take a few seconds or a few minutes. Your goal is not to get rid of the feeling but to make peace with it.

How long? How often? Every time unpleasant feelings arise, you can do this exercise.

Tips & Tricks:

- **Fighting is useless.** Nobody wants to have unpleasant feelings. We want to get away as soon as possible. Unfortunately, that doesn't work. The more we fight these feelings, like fear or anger, the stronger they become. That's why the only way is to make peace with them

- **The key is to let your feelings be there.** The aim of this exercise is not to fight and destroy unpleasant emotions but to let them be there. By making peace with them, they disappear on their own.

- **Thief in the empty house**. There is a Buddhist metaphor: the negative feeling is like a thief in an empty house. The thief comes into the house; we don't stop him. We'll just let him be there. The thief sees that there is nothing valuable in this house and just leaves.

Let's see how Lara uses this exercise. Her child is sick,

and she is worried.

1. Observe: Lara's thoughts are circling. She focuses her attention on the corresponding body sensations: Lara feels pressure and vibrations in the solar plexus. She tries to concentrate on it. She asks herself where the body sensation occurs. This strengthens her concentration.

2. Breathe: Lara breathes deeply into the body sensation. That calms her down. The worried thoughts diminish. Also the worried body sensations lessen.

3. Allow: Lara allows the feeling to be there -- she gives it space. The resistance against the unpleasant body sensations decreases. The sensations become softer and weaker. After a while, the worries are gone.

That's it with intensity level one. In the next chapter we look at the next intensity level.

Managing moderately intense emotions with the latest tactics

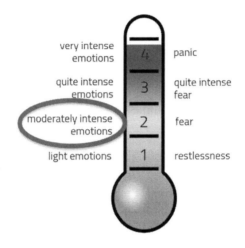

very intense emotions — 4 — panic

quite intense emotions — 3 — quite intense fear

moderately intense emotions — 2 — fear

light emotions — 1 — restlessness

We're at intensity two. At this intensity, the feeling is stronger. As I said, in the end, your subjective feeling counts how intense or disturbing you think the feeling is. For example, mild anger can have intensity one, anger intensity two, rage intensity three, and furious anger intensity four.

At this intensity, we work with two techniques and you can decide for yourself which one suits you better. The first technique is a breathing exercise. It is scientifically very well investigated and helps excellently with fears and panic. It's the 4-7-8 breath.

"The strongest and most effective anti-anxiety measure I know is the 4-7-8 breath technique. I've seen it work on the most extreme forms of panic disorder when the strongest medications have failed." – Dr. Weil

Breathing techniques work very well to alleviate emotions, whether it's fear or anger. The good thing about breathing techniques is that they work automatically. The body is signaled by the calm breathing to weaken the feeling. We use the breathing technique here to nip them in the bud every time negative thoughts or feelings appear. This means that the more mindful we are, the more we notice a negative thought or a negative feeling in the beginning. That's what we call baby feelings. This is much easier to keep in check than a full-grown feeling. The 4-7-8 breath serves as a disrupter. We focus our attention away from our negative thoughts to breathing. That way we can't even get into a cycle of thoughts. Our system will quickly calm down, and negative thoughts and feelings will disappear.

"The benefits are gradual and cumu-

lative, which ultimately leads to better health for the entire nervous system. It is also a specific treatment for hypertension, cold hands, irritable bowel syndrome, arrhythmia, anxiety and panic disorders, and a variety of other common conditions. Above all, it is the most effective and time-efficient relaxation method I have found." – Dr. Weil

---

4-7-8 breath

Goal: thought stopping and relaxation

Technique:

1. Touch your palate with the tip of your tongue just behind your upper incisors. Keep your tongue in this position throughout your breathing.

2. Exhale completely through your mouth and lips with a "woosh" sound, like you want to blow out a candle.

3. Close your mouth and **inhale** silently through your nose, **counting to four**.

4. **Hold** your breath **counting to seven**.

5. **Exhale** through your mouth like you did in step two, **counting to eight**.

Repeat steps three, four, and five for a total of four

breaths.

How often? How long? At least twice a day. Moreover, use this every time negative thoughts or feelings arise. For the first four weeks, do not take more than four breaths each. After that, you're welcome to do more but not more than eight.

Tips & Tricks:

- **Effective against stress and anxiety**: This breathing technique was propagated by Dr. Andrew Weil. It's a great remedy for anxiety and stress. Performed daily, this respiration has other positive effects, such as a significant drop in blood pressure or lowering the average heart rate. This breathing technique is so effective that it works even better against anxiety and panic attacks than medication. It is a simple and very effective relaxing breathing technique.

- **In the morning and in the evening**: You can use the breathing method at any time. Dr. Weil himself recommends it in the morning after waking up and in the evening before going to bed.

- **Sleep in one minute**: The breathing method is known to let you fall asleep in one minute. So, if you have sleep problems, this technique is the best help.

- **Explanation video**: Dr. Weil explains the breathing technique in a video under the following link: https://bit.ly/2qS0Dkd.

John has a quarrel with his girlfriend: "I just need my peace! I just walked in the door, I really don't want to take out the garbage," he scolds his girlfriend, Lisa. She is hurt and repsonds: "Don't be so lazy! That only takes two minutes! Come on, move your ass!" John gets more and more annoyed. He already wants to snap at Lisa, but he stops there. He is mindful for a short moment and thinks: "No, it's not worth arguing about something like that. I have to calm down!" He says: "Lisa, wait, I have to go to the toilet for a moment, then we'll talk again, ok?" Lisa keeps her mouth open, and John quickly disappears to the toilet. There he practices 4-7-8 breath four times. He feels his anger give way and becomes relaxed. Lisa is still waiting in the hallway. She immediately sees that something has changed, and her posture becomes softer. "Hey honey, I'm taking the garbage down right now, okay?" he informs her. Lisa's eyes widen, she grabs his hand and purrs: "No, do it later, rest for a while."

Did you like this technique? It works very quickly. The next technique we are going to look at is defusion. Here we allow negative thoughts, but do not believe them.

Defusion

What is defusion? Let us first look at the word fusion. What is merging here? We had noticed that negative feelings arise from negative thoughts. But that's not the whole story. Negative thoughts do not always lead to negative feelings. The crucial point is whether we believe in our negative thoughts or not. If we believe our negative thoughts, negative feelings arise. Therefore, thoughts and feelings merge. And we don't want that. Thoughts in themselves are not negative. No, they're just words or pictures in our heads. Suffering only arises when we believe in our thoughts.

Charles had an interview. It didn't go very well. Charles immediately began to belittle himself: "I am such a loser! I'll never get a job!" Because of these negative thoughts and because Charles believed them, he immediately felt bad. He called his girlfriend, and she appeased him: "Charles, such things happen. You're only human! I don't know anyone who hasn't screwed up at an interview before. I'm sure the next one will be better." She made him not believe his disparaging statements, "I am a failure!" Charles thus gained distance from his thoughts. He defused his thoughts and feelings and felt better.

Defusion means that we bring distance between our thoughts and feelings. We break the connection between our thoughts and feelings.

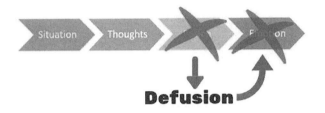

The figure illustrates this. In the above example, the situation is the interview that did not go well. Karl then had the thought: "I am a failure!" Most people automatically believe their thoughts. This means that thoughts and emotions fuse. From the thought "I am a loser" comes the emotion of frustration. Karl's girl-friend made him not believe the thought. This is a de-fusion. So the thought does not lead to any emotion — the frustration is gone, and Karl can deal with the situation calmly.

A well-known defusion technique is that we let our voices speak in our heads like Mickey Mouse. Imagine how it would be if Mickey Mouse said to you in your head: "You are a failure!" Not so bad - right? This is an example of a defusion technique. I'll introduce you to some more below. They all come from ACT (Attention and Commitment Therapy).

Source:
https://www.deviantart.com/zdrer456/art/Mickey-Mouse-196130127

This is a very modern and effective form of therapy. It belongs to the third wave of behavioral therapies. The **first wave** was pure behavioral therapies. We only worked on the behavior. That means, for example, if someone is afraid of heights, he was first only allowed to climb a few steps of a tower, later a few more, etc. until he could climb the entire tower. This means that the therapists at that time were solely concerned with the patients' behavior. His thoughts and beliefs were ignored.

This changed with ingenious therapists like Aaron Beck and Albert Ellis. In the fifties and sixties they developed the **second wave** of behavioral therapy.

They postulated that negative feelings arise from negative thoughts. And that is why thoughts must be examined and their power diminished. The resulting forms of therapy were summarized under the term cognitive behavior therapy.

In the **third wave** of behavioral therapy, elements of Buddhism were added. MBSR (Mindfulness-Based Stress Reduction) by Jon Kabatt-Zin is one example. The ACT also belongs to the third wave.

I call thoughts words or pictures in your head. The defusion techniques are suitable for words as well as for inner images. First, I'll introduce you to some techniques for meeting negative inner statements. Then I'll give you effective techniques to manage negative inner images.

Defusion Techniques I (Words)

Goal: to gain distance from negative thoughts

Technique:

1. Musical thoughts: The voice in your head proclaims: "I am a failure!" How do you feel about that? Now sing this statement to the song "Happy Birthday." In my experience, you just can't take sung thoughts seriously anymore. Of course, you can use any other song.

2. Name your stories: This is a somewhat more demanding technique, but it is very effective. We always tell each other the same stories. There aren't too many of them, maybe four or five. The technique is to give the stories a title. This alleviates the power of thought. It also leads to more self-knowledge. Many are surprised how often we tell each other the same story over and over again.

My friend Fabian liked to tell himself the story: "I'm not good enough!" This story appeared in countless variations. For example, when he met a woman, the voice in his head would say, "She looks far too good for you. You don't stand a chance with her!" Fabian now began to call such thoughts "not-good enough story." That distanced him from his thoughts.

3. Beeping voice: Another technique in defusion is the "beeping voice." Here you say the negative thoughts in a funny voice. You can take the voice of Mickey Mouse, Bart Simpson, or you can take an erotic voice. Of course, you can choose any other voice that is pleasant for you. The main thing is to defuse the negative thought.

4. Thank your thought: You may simply say to your talkative Darth Vader "thanks, dear mind" or "thanks! That is very informative." However, you should not speak aggressively or sarcastically to your mind. Warm and humorous is the right approach. Your talkative Darth Vader doesn't mean any harm.

How long? How often? Use these techniques any time you notice negative thoughts. You do this until you distance yourself from your thoughts, even without these techniques.

Tips & Tricks:

- **Thoughts are just words strung together**: The goal is for you to recognize that thoughts are just words. Thoughts in themselves are not a threat. So you don't have to get rid of negative thoughts, which is not possible; no, you just have to defuse them.
- **Observer role**: The techniques presented here have the final goal that you simply gain distance from your thoughts and that you slip into an observer role. Once you've done that, you don't even need to use the defusion techniques anymore, or at least only occasionally.
- **Alternatively or combined**: You can use the defusion techniques alternatively. You choose the one you like best. I am, for example, a fan of "Name your thoughts" defusion. It is powerful and gives me valuable insights. Or you can use them in combination: one technique once, then another.
- **A bit of drama is quite nice**: By the way, the stories and negative thoughts will always be there. This is part of our life here on Earth. Get over it. On the other hand, if we didn't have negative thoughts, wouldn't that be boring? Imagine watching a movie and all people are just nice to each other. Nobody misunderstands anything; nobody insinuates evil inten-

tions. Where's the drama? Wouldn't this movie be boring as hell?

Do you already have a favorite? Which of the defusion techniques did you like best? Below are the promised techniques for inner images.

Defusion Techniques II (Images)

Goal: to gain distance from negative inner images

Technique:

1. Screen: Recall a negative inner image. Maybe the last time you had a big fight with your partner. Or when your boss criticized you. Feel what that feels like. Now imagine a screen in the other corner of the room. You project this image onto this screen. Now play with the picture. You can turn it around, run it in slow motion, or in black and white. There are no limits to your imagination. Now feel how your feeling changes to this inner image.

2. Funny subtitles or comments: You can add funny comments to your inner image or movies. For example: "The epic quarrel, broadcast next Friday on FOX." If you have already given this story a name, you can use it. Try to be playful and humorous. See how that makes you feel.

3. Music: You can add music to your inner movie. See what works best: rock, jazz, hip hop, or classical music. Be playful and keen to experiment.

4. Fantasy without limits: You are God in your inner image or film. You can do anything. You can make yourself look huge and your boss tiny as an ant. You can do anything. There are no limits to your imagination. For example, you can imagine the boss taking you down, and the mouse police will come and pick him up. Of course your boss is also small as a mouse. The only important thing is to defuse your inner image.

How long? How often? Use these techniques anytime you have an unpleasant picture or inner film.

Tips & Tricks:

- **Therapist**: The techniques presented are very effective. However, please be careful with very traumatic memories, such as rape, torture, or domestic violence. You should work on these together with a therapist.
- **Combination of several techniques**: You can also use the techniques together. So if you have a negative image in your head, first apply the first technique, then the second, third, and fourth techniques. Or you can choose one or two techniques that you particularly like.
- **Prevention for stubborn images**: If the inner image is still unpleasant or frightening for you, I recommend applying the above techniques to the image for five minutes a day for a week. That is, even if the image did not appear, you

take five minutes extra daily to defuse the image. So you work preventively with the inner images.

That was intensity level two. I have introduced you to two very different techniques, and I am curious which you like better.

Quite intense emotion control: new generation techniques

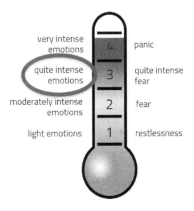

At the "quite intense" level, things are already getting down to business. Our talkative Darth Vader already has a really big mouth here.

Light emotions, for example, would be "restlessness." "Worry" would be the next step, namely moderate intense feelings. "Fear" is quite an intense feeling. The most intense emotion is panic.

This chapter would then be responsible for "fear". I'll

introduce you to two very strong techniques. The first is the Delete Button. It is a technique from the family of thought stopping techniques.

By adding some ingredients, this becomes the new improved generation of thought-stopping techniques, the thought-stop turbo, so to speak. Then I'll introduce you to the Sedona method. Hundreds of thousands of people have been able to free themselves from their unpleasant thoughts and feelings with this method. That is why it should not be missing in this book.

The Delete Button

Goal: thought stopping and relaxation

Technique:

1. Imagine a button in the middle of your chest or

palm that simply turns off thinking.

2. Breathe in and out three deep breaths into your stomach. Count the breaths and imagine a different color each time.

3. Now press the button and imagine that your mind is completely empty. Make a move with one hand as if you are really pressing a button.

4. Focus your attention on the next two breaths and bring your attention back to the present moment.

How often? How long? Do this exercise every time negative thoughts or feelings arise.

Tips & Tricks:

- **Baby feelings**: Try to notice the negative thoughts or feelings at the beginning of their emergence. The smaller the thoughts and feelings are, the easier we can fight them.
- **Thought stop turbo**: Compared to the classic thought stopping exercise, this improved version is much more effective. In the classic thought stopping exercise you simply think the word "stop." With the Delete Button, we pay attention to our breath, imagine colors, and visualize a delete button. In addition, we make a small movement: we actually press the delete key. All this combined makes for the enormous effect.

Karsten suffered from anxiety. He was afraid of diseases. At the moment, he was afraid of larynx cancer. His thoughts revolved around this fear so that he touched his larynx several times a day. Although he found nothing there, it did not reassure him. I advised him to use the Delete key every time a fearful thought or feeling arose. He reported: "Yesterday, I was already lying in bed, and the fear came again. I could not perceive the thoughts, but the emotion. I was mindful and so I caught the fear when it was not yet so strong. I breathed deeply in and out and imagined the color blue. It is reassuring for me. Then I breathed deeply in and out of my belly a second time. I imagined the color red. With the third breath, I took the color orange. The fear was still there, but already weaker. Then I imagined how I pressed the button in the middle of my chest. At the same time, I actually made the corresponding hand movement, as if there was actually a button there. Surprisingly, I actually had the impression that suddenly all my thoughts had disappeared. I felt more peaceful right away. Two more breaths into my stomach, and my fear was almost gone! It was great! "That makes me very happy! You did well," I praised him. Karsten continued: "Today the fear appeared three times. The first time immediately after waking up. That was very unpleasant. I forgot in the confusion to use the technique, and the fear caught me completely. Luckily, the next two times I could press the delete button again, which was very helpful." "You did very well anyway. It happens that one forgets to use the technique -- especially at the beginning. The essential thing about this technique is that you stay with it. You really should use the delete button every single time the fear appears. The more often you do that, the more likely the fear disappears completely. But endurance is very important here," I explained.

Now we come to the famous Sedona method. Buckle up; it's gonna be a wild ride. Well, it's not that wild, but I wanted to say that this technique is really good. The central goal of this technique is to let go.

Sedona method

Goal: to let go of negative thoughts and emotions

Technique:

Ask yourself the following four questions:

1. Could I accept this feeling right now?

2. Could I let go of this feeling just for this moment?

3. Would I let go of this feeling?

4. When?

How long? How often? You can use this technique anytime negative thoughts or feelings arise. So it's an in-between technique. However, you can also use it as a prophylaxis in a quiet minute.

Tips & Tricks:

- **From your heart**: Answer every question

from your heart. Don't think too long. Your answer is surprisingly not that important. You can't do anything wrong.

- **Repeat**: Repeat the questions! You can repeat the questions until you actually let go of the feeling. Often the four questions already work the first time. My experience is that I often have to repeat the four questions several times according to the intensity of the feeling.

- **There is no wrong answer**: You are free to answer the questions. I don't want to influence you, but I answer "yes" to the first question and "no" to the second. The third I affirm again and at the fourth...see below.

- **Loud or noiseless**: You can think about this technique or you can practice it out loud. It works a little better out loud.

- The standard answer to question four "when?" is "now!" You can say "now" energetically or even really loudly. Let it convince you for yourself.

- **It even works without an answer**: By the way, you don't have to answer the question. The questions work the same way. But if you have time, I suggest you answer it.

- **Short form**: You can also make the whole technique as a short form. Then omit the first question and ask yourself:

1. Could I let go of the feeling?

2. Would I?

3. When?

You don't always have enough time. If this is the case or if you are already very familiar with the process, you can use this short form.

All right so far? In the following I will go even deeper into the questions and their mode of action:

Explanations to the questions

Can I accept that feeling right now?

Acceptance is always a good idea. When we fight a feeling, it gets stronger. Acceptance means that we give room to the feeling. This is not always easy, especially when the feeling is unpleasant. When I'm afraid, I want the fear to go away. Inviting the fear doesn't look like a good idea. Fortunately, the question is only about accepting for a brief moment. We can do this, can't we? My answer to this question is always a "yes." Because, in fact, I can accept any feeling for a brief moment. This immediately soften emotions, and they fade away a little.

Could I let go of this feeling now?

Like all questions, we should answer from our hearts. Don't think too long. It's not always so easy to let go. Sometimes I can let go of an emotion easily, sometimes not. Everything's all right. Every answer is fine. Nevertheless, this question works. Our system is given the impulse to let go. It works subtly.

Would I let go of this feeling?

Well, what can one answer? Of course I want to let go of that feeling. This question reinforces the impetus given by the previous question.

When?

I answer this question every time with an energetic "now!" That is the real purpose of this question. We are being brought back to the here and now.

Two ways to use the Sedona method: The Sedona method is flexible. We can use it either acutely or preventively:

1. Let go of current negative thoughts and feelings: Every time a negative feeling or thought arises, we can use the Sedona method. Suppose your partner is angry with you right now and accuses you of unfairness. You get angry, too, and there's a big fight. You can use the Sedona method in this situation instead. Best use the short form: "Could I let go of the trouble? Would I? When?" You can do this in your mind so that your partner doesn't notice. You'll see your anger fading fast. Take a few rounds with the Sedona method until your anger has subsided.

You can also take a little break. Tell your partner you need to go to the bathroom. There apply the short form of the Sedona method. Drink a glass of water or do some breathing exercises. Your anger will go away quickly.

2. Let go of your emotions preventively: *Sara's still hurt because of her ex-boyfriend Mark. He cheated on her with her best friend. This thing happened two years ago, but every time Sara thinks about it, she feels angry and hurt. She just can't forgive Mark and her former best friend. In this situation, I advised Sara to use the Sedona method in writing. The first step was for Sara to write down all her thoughts, upsets, and complaints on the subject. I told her not to mince matters. Sara wrote down a lot of statements, some of them very energetic. For example, she wrote: "Mark's a fucking asshole!" With this sentence, Sara started to feel anger and rage. She now applied the Sedona method. She had to repeat the four questions many times until her anger died down. She then applied the Sedona method to all her statements. The whole procedure took about an hour. Already after this one session Sara felt considerably liberated. She did this several more times until she was completely freed from these feelings of anger and hurt.*

Just like Sara, you can use the Sedona method in writing. This means that you take a theme from your life and write down the corresponding beliefs and statements that you have. For each statement, apply the Sedona method until you let go of the negative feelings and thoughts. You will be surprised how well this method works.

If you work prophylactically, I recommend using the Sedona method in writing. In addition, you can apply the method to other occasions, like when you drive to work. Meanwhile, you can easily edit your topics with the four questions.

How to control very intense emotions

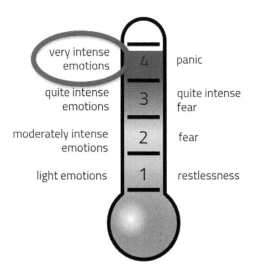

Now we've reached intensity level four. This refers to feelings that are particularly strong, such as panic or strong rage. These feelings can be overwhelming. It can happen that we cannot get a reasonable grip on the emotions in the situation itself. For example, we give free rein to our fury and insult and hurt our partner. That is why I recommend that we work preventively here. That is, when the emotion is not there right now, you work on it. This will soften it, and you can deal with it better when it is acute.

Alex is a spirited guy. He's been with his girlfriend An-
na for five years. It's a good relationship in itself, but
the fights are scary. They both scream and insult each
other. Afterwards both are very hurt and even think
about splitting up. "Anna just knows my sore spots!
She's pushing my buttons! I get so angry I'd like to
throw her out the window." Of course, it would be nice
if Alex could stay calm. For example, he could do the 4-
7-8 breath. Unfortunately, this is not so easy in prac-
tice. When the feelings are so persistent and intense,
Alex should work preventively.

That means here we combine two techniques. On the
one hand, a preventive technique and on the other
hand an acute technique:

- The **preventive technique is *The Work*:** This
  is a great and incredibly effective method. This
  technique is very similar to the ABCDE method. I described the ABCDE method in detail in
  my book *Stress is an Illusion.* The method I
  present now is called The Work. This method
  works with four questions and an inversion.
- In addition to The Work, you use another
  technique for the **acute** situation. For example,
  you can combine The Work with the Sedona
  method or with the 4-7-8 breath.

First, I'll introduce The Work to you in detail. It was
developed by Byron Katie. She suffered from severe
anxiety and depression, so severe that she could
hardly leave her bed. According to her own state-

ments, she had an enlightenment experience that completely freed her from fear and depression. To give inner peace to other people, she developed The Work.

Quelle: https://blog.bulletproof.com/byron-katie-532/

This method is incredibly effective. After the first application, you will notice a difference.

The Work

Goal: dissolving negative thoughts

Technique:

Step 1: The first step is to find out what our beliefs and negative thoughts are about the situation. There is a worksheet for this. This worksheet asks you questions. Answer it as if no one would ever read it. It is important that you judge uninhibitedly. This contributes to the effectiveness of this method. By the way, it is also important that you answer these questions in writing. If we do this in our heads, too much is simply lost. Written, on the other hand, we are much more concentrated.

Spreadsheet:

- Who or what annoys you; what makes you sad or disappointed?
- What exactly is it that you didn't like or still don't like?
- How should he/she/it change? What do you want from him/her?
- What exactly should he/she do, be, think, or feel?
- Do you need anything from him/her? What should he/she give you or do for you to be happy?
- What do you think about him/her? Make a list.

Let's see what Alex answered to those questions:

- Who or what annoys you; what makes you sad or disappointed? *What pisses me off is that Anna knows no boundaries. She insults me where she can. She doesn't respect me at all.*
- What exactly is it that you didn't like or still don't like? *She always makes a mountain out of a molehill. That's terrible. She's always fighting.*
- How should he/she/it change? What do you want from him/her? *I want her to listen to me. I want us to have a fair and quiet fight. It*

71

shouldn't get loud, damn it!

- What exactly should he/she do, be, think, or feel? *Anna should realize what a good boyfriend I am. She should appreciate me and not treat me so badly.*
- Do you need anything from him/her? What should he/she give you or do for you to be happy? *She should listen to me. She should stay calm and respond to what I'm saying. She shouldn't always think negatively so quickly.*
- What do you think about him/her? Make a list. *She's not listening. She's trying to hurt me really bad. She's getting loud. She gets furious terribly quickly. She doesn't respect me. She's always criticizing me.*

Step 2: In the next step, we ask four questions about each of these statements and make a turnaround. That sounds like a lot of work at first glance. But it's not. Often it is sufficient to work intensively on two or three statements. The rest is self-evident.

Let's take the statement *"Anna doesn't respect me"* because it happened several times. The first question we ask ourselves is:

1. Is that true? We go within ourselves and answer from our hearts. We do not give a quick answer of the mind, but we let this question work on us.

Alex replied: "Of course it's true!" Every answer is correct. This is not about censoring or finding the right

72

answer.

2. Do you really know it's true? You're right, it's the same question again. This is because we tend to answer the first question too quickly.

The second question had a greater impact on Alex. He said: "Well, actually I can't really know. I'd have to be able to read her mind. There are also many situations in which she treats me very respectfully and well. Apart from our fights, she's very friendly and courteous. If she didn't respect me, she probably wouldn't be with me. So I can't know she doesn't respect me."

As an alternative question, you might ask: **Where is the proof?** If you're not sure, consider if twelve witnesses had seen Anna's behavior, would they all have come to the conclusion that Anna treats Alex disrespectfully?

The first two questions are about softening our negative thoughts a little. A fusion occurs when we believe our negative thought. By asking, "Is this thought really true?" we let ourselves doubt the truth. Maybe that thought isn't true at all. Just between you and me, most negative thoughts are not true. If you do The Work more often, you will most likely come to the same conclusion.

3. How do I react to this thought? What do we feel, and how do we act when we think of this thought?

"How does Alex react to the idea that Anna doesn't respect him?" This means feelings and actions. Alex is

73

annoyed when he thinks that Anna treats him disre-
spectfully. Then he quickly gets loud, and out of his in-
jury, he tries to hurt Anna as well.

The turnaround

With the first two questions we can see that our negative thoughts are not true. Question three and four
lead us to the realization that not the situation, but
our negative thoughts make us feel bad. The turnaround goes one step further: our negative thoughts
are reversed here. We realize that the opposite of our
negative thoughts is true. Let's look at Alex's example. There are several ways of turning around:

1. Is the opposite true?

The opposite is: "Anna respects me!" Is that true? Yes!
There are many situations in which Anna treats Alex
very affectionately and positively. She respects him.
The fact that she is angry with him in the event of a
dispute and even gets loud does not mean that she does
not respect him.

2. Insert yourself:

Instead of saying "Anna doesn't respect me!" the inver-
sion is "I don't respect myself!" When you turn it
around, always ask yourself if it is more true than the
original statement. In fact, Alex doesn't respect himself.
Why? Because he has negative thoughts that harm
himself. Sometimes you have to be creative and think
figuratively when reversing. However, not every
turnaround makes sense. It may also be that an in-

version just doesn't feel good.

3. Use my thinking:

Here the reversal is: *"My thinking does not respect me!" In this case, it is similar to the previous reversal. Is this inversion more true than the original statement? Yes! Anna's behavior towards Alex is only disrespect by Alex's interpretation. Only by the thought "Anna treats me disrespectfully" the disrespect arises. Alex could also think, for example, "I hurt Anna. She's defending herself. I'm sorry about that." Thoughts create disrespect. So this turnaround is truer.*

4. Mix-up:

The turnaround is, *"Alex doesn't respect Anna!" Is that truer than the original statement? Yes! Alex doesn't treat Anna with respect either. He's loud to her, angry, and unforgiving.*

You don't always have to do all four turnarounds. It is enough if we find one that seems truer to us than the original statement. The reversal should touch us and make us realize how one-sidedly we have judged the situation. It should cause an "a-ha" effect.

How often? How long? The Work is a method that we do not apply acutely. However, if you have a lot of experience with it, acute application is also possible. Otherwise you should use The Work daily for at least one to three weeks. After that, whenever the negative feeling occurs. Until you are freed from that intense negative feeling.

Tips & Tricks:

- **Written**: The Work is really a great method. It leads to inner peace. You should use it regularly. Important: it must be in writing!

- **Answer questions freshly**: The questions should not be answered mechanically. I know from my own experience: If you have more experience with The Work, you tend to answer the questions quickly because you know the answers already. I know most of the time that the negative thought isn't true. And I know the negative thought brings me to the negative feelings. Nevertheless, we should always answer the questions freshly, as if it were the first time.

- **Can I control it?** Ask this question as the fifth question! It's very effective. It does not belong to the original The Work, but it is a useful addition. The following example describes how you deal with this question.

- **Three examples of the turnaround**: In addition, you can find three examples of the turnaround that support the respective turnaround. This increases the effect of the inversion. An inversion of Alex is "I don't respect Anna!" Alex looked for three examples. He quickly found it: "I was loud to her. I insulted and abused her." If you find three examples, you can be sure that the inversion is more true than the original negative thought.

Let's look at another example.

The negative thought is:

"My boss should recognize me more and praise me."

You can add a fifth question if you like. And that is: "Can I control this?" You can formulate this directly as the first question. Let's take a closer look.

The Greek philosopher Epictetus wrote almost 2,000 years ago in his *Handbook Of Morality*:

"In our power stands our thinking, our doing, our desire, our dislike, in short: everything that comes from ourselves. Not in our power is our body, our possessions, our prestige, our external position — in a word, everything that does not come from ourselves."

That means we can't control what others do. External factors such as the weather, the stock market, traffic, etc. are not in our power either. Why is it important to know this? When we realize that we can't control what other people do, we can be at peace with it.

Alex can't control Anna. It's her thoughts, feelings, and

actions. Alex can't control her getting loud with him. Asked, "Can I control that?", Alex realizes once again that he has no influence.

Wanting to control something over which we have no control only causes us stress. Don't we all want a stress-free life? If so, we should not be upset when other people do something they should not do. Okay, back to our example:

1. Can I control it? I*t's in my boss's power. I can't control my boss. He has a mind of his own. It's good to know when we can and can't do something.* If we know that it is not in our power, we can accept it more easily and be at peace with it. That is why this question is so valuable.

2. Is it true? And where's the proof? *Is it really true that my boss should recognize and praise me more? Where's the proof? Is there a law that obliges bosses to praise and acknowledge their employees? No! Reality tells us many bosses don't praise. However, our boss acknowledges us very well because he pays our salaries. That's a credit too. So we conclude, "It's not true."*

3. Can I really know that it would be better if my boss praised and acknowledged me? Here we have changed the question a little. We can do that very well with "should" sentences. If it's not a "should" phrase, then we ask the usual question: "Can I really know for 100 percent that it's true?"

Would it really be better? Maybe yes, maybe no. I'd feel

better here and there if my boss praised me. Since we don't see each other that often, and he has a lot of other things to do, he wouldn't be able to praise me very much anyway. I'd be happy if he did, but it doesn't make much difference.

4. How do I react to this thought? *I'm angry with my boss. I don't feel recognized enough. That demotivates me.*

5. Who would I be without this thought? *I'd just be in the here and now. I would do my job and not think about my boss owing me anything. I could see my boss as the kind of person he is. He's doing a good job on the whole.*

The turnaround:

"My boss shouldn't acknowledge and praise me." Is this truer? Yes. Because he doesn't. Every time we fight reality, we lose and that leads to stress. In fact, I don't know if it would really be better for me if he praised me. It doesn't really matter.

"I should acknowledge myself and praise myself." Is that true? Of course! I can't control my boss, but I can control myself. If I would praise and acknowledge myself more, then I would no longer need the praise of my boss.

"I should praise and appreciate my boss more." Is that true? I often condemn my boss in my thoughts. I'm taking him down. I would actually feel better if I recognized my boss more.

Another example:

The negative thought is,

"I'll die from my panic."

1. Is it true? And where is the proof? *Many people suffer from panic. No one has ever died because of it. That is also not the purpose of panic; panic is supposed to protect us from dangerous situations, i.e., if a tiger jumps out of the bush and threatens our life, we should have enough energy to flee from him. That is panic. It is a survival program. So the result is exactly the opposite of death. We conclude therefore: "It is not true."*

2. Is it really true? *No! If we came to this conclusion already in the first question, we don't need to answer the second one again.*

3. How do I react to this thought? *We develop a fear of panic. That makes things even worse. We are restless and anxious*

4. Who would I be without this thought? *I would simply be in the here and now. I would not be afraid of panic. I would live now. All in all, I would be more relaxed.*

The turnaround:

Here, the turnaround that fits best is "I won't die" because this is more true than the original statement. Panic is a survival program, not a dying one.

I hope the examples has brought you closer to the

method. It is really worth using this method. Would you like to know more? The following books and links are great:

- **In YouTube,** there are many videos worth seeing. I highly recommend videos by Byron Katie. She is the founder of The Work. Just type "Byron Katie" into the search field of Youtube, and you will get countless great videos.

- **You like more to read?** Then I recommend this book from Byron Katie: *Loving What Is.*

In a nutshell

- With light feelings you can manage excellently with acceptance. Acceptance means that we give the feeling space and allow it.

- For moderately intense emotions you can work with the soothing 4-7-8 breath. Scientifically proven, it works excellently against anxiety. Alternatively, you can use different defusion techniques. They just make you stop taking your negative thoughts seriously.

- You fight quite intense emotions with the Sedona method. It consists of four questions and helps you let go of your feelings. Instead, you can work with the technique of the Delete Button. This is an improved version of the thought stopping technique.

- Very intense feelings, such as panic, should be

treated prophylactically and acutely. You use
The Work when the feeling isn't there right
now. You do this for about one to three weeks.
For acute situations you choose one of the
other techniques.

The revolutionary
5-step peace process

"We all have the power to be happy
under any circumstances."
– Byron Katie

In this chapter...

- The 5-step peace process shows you exactly how to apply the techniques and how to proceed most effectively.
- It's a step-by-step guide that teaches you how to control your emotions.

You've learned a lot of techniques so far. What's the best way to deal with this? I have designed a step-by-step guide for this. It has proven itself and is extremely effective.

5-step peace process

1) Determine the intensity and frequency: What intensity and frequency has the unpleasant feeling you want to deal with?

Do you remember Sara? She had to struggle to forgive her ex-boyfriend Mark. Her irreconcilability was persistent. She had to think about it every day. She then felt annoyed and hurt and classified the intensity as "moderately intense." If an unpleasant feeling is very persistent or very intense, it is always a consideration to use The Work.

2. Selection and application of techniques: Think about the techniques you want to use. The intensity and persistence of the feeling gives you clues.

Frequency / Intensity	rare (several times a week)	occasionally (at least 1 x per day)	**often** (several times/frequently per day)	permanent (several times per hour)
1 = light	Expansion	Expansion	Expansion	Expansion
2 = moderate	Defusion/ 4-7-8 Breath	Defusion/ 4-7-8 Breath	Defusion/ 4-7-8 Breath	Defusion/ 4-7-8 Breath
3 = quite	Sedona/ Delete Button	Sedona/ Delete Button	Sedona/ Delete Button	TheWork
4 = very	Sedona/ Delete Button	TheWork	TheWork	TheWork

If you have some experience, always pay attention to your intuition. Suppose you experience an unpleasant feeling in the intensity of four, but your intuition says that the Delete Key fits best. Then try it out. Otherwise, I suggest first trying out the techniques that are intended for this intensity and frequency.

How long should you use the techniques? Until the emotions are gone or you can accept them. But also have a look in the next chapter where there is a detailed explanation of how long you should use the techniques.

3. When and what circumstances? Identify exactly when and under which circumstances this unpleasant feeling occurs. This is important! Use an app or notepad and write down exactly in which situation and at what time the feeling occurs. I know, it's annoying. I ask you to do it anyway, if only for a few days. Writing it down has some important advantages:

- On the one hand, it can shed light on the causes. Maybe your anxiety always comes after you go to the gym. This can indicate that you are perhaps training too intensively and thus putting too much stress on your body.
- Second, you're getting more mindful. You now know in which situations your negative feelings occur. This attracts your attention, so you don't react automatically. What do I mean by that? Negative feelings are usually automatic. You enter a situation, negative thoughts automatically arise, you fuse with this thought, and the negative feeling appears. This process has become a habit. This is what happens over and over again. That's why you first have to create the awareness to not react automatically.

If the unpleasant feeling has a maximum intensity of three and does not occur frequently at the same time, the process can already be over here. Just make sure that you apply the respective technique in the respective situation. Nevertheless, I would like to refer you to step five. This is about additional resources.

4. The Work: This step is optional. You should only do it when the feeling is at an intensity of three or four. Here's what you do:

a) Identify your negative thoughts: This means that you must first find out which negative thoughts and beliefs appear in the corresponding situation. The worksheet helps to do this.

Worksheet

- Who or what annoys you; what makes you sad or disappointed?
- What exactly is it that you didn't like or still don't like?
- How should he/she/it change? What do you want from him/her?
- What exactly should he/she do, be, think, or feel?
- Do you need anything from him/her? What should he/she give you or do for you to be happy?
- What do you think about him/her? Make a list.

b) Do The Work daily for one to three weeks: After you have found out your beliefs and negative thoughts, you work on them daily with The Work for a week. You don't always have to work on every single negative thought. Take out the ones that are strongest. Then do The Work for a week. It's no problem if you work on the same beliefs over and over again every day. The important thing is that you don't do it mechanically. Listen to yourself again and again; feel what your truth is. After a week, you'll see how your feelings have changed. The Work is very powerful. You may not have to work with The Work after this week. If the unpleasant feeling you are working on is still very intense and persistent, add another week. You can repeat this for up to three weeks. After that, the intensity of the feeling should really have subsided. Then you either reduce The Work to once a week or omit it completely. Then go to step one and re-evaluate your feelings.

c) Supplementary technique: Still choose another technique besides The Work. You then apply these in the acute situation.

We had Alex's example. He had an anger problem. Since the feeling was very intense, he did The Work preventively. In the acute situation itself, it is difficult to do The Work. That's why Alex chose another technique to complement The Work. 4-7-8 breath is ideal for tantrums. Alex chose this technique. By the way, all techniques except expansion are suitable for intense emotions.

d) Additional Resources: This step is also optional. In many situations there are valuable additional resources that we can use. For example, we can join a self-help group on this topic or if we have depression, it is an excellent idea to exercise. There are also many interesting energetic techniques, such as EFT or energetically based breathing techniques. There are many resources that can help us. We should use them.

The 5-step peace process is the framework within

which you use the techniques to control your emotions. In the next chapter, we will apply this process to some important emotions.

How long should the techniques be used?

I have to do a little explanation for that. Negative thoughts are often persistent. Why? Because they've become a habit like brushing your teeth. We have to be patient enough to change habits. It was thought that you had to repeat an action for 21 days to form a habit. Unfortunately, that's not true. Recent studies have shown that a habit takes between 18 and 254 days to develop. On average, a habit forms after 66 days. How long it takes for an action to become a habit depends above all on how difficult and costly it is. For example, it is more difficult to establish one hour of jogging as a habit than watching 10 minutes of television. Our body is programmed to save as much energy as possible. This is a program from our prehistory, in which food shortages were still part of everyday life. Wherever possible, energy had to be saved. That's why watching TV for 10 minutes is easier than jogging for an hour.

This means, for example: You have to jog an average of 66 days in a row, then it's a habit. Once it's a habit, you don't have to make any effort. Your brain rather signals to you: "If I don't jog today, I feel strange. I have to go out and jog in a minute." Daily jogging is with you now. If you don't, you feel weird. It's a habit.

For us, this means that we have to use a technique for at least 18 days to break down our habit of producing negative thoughts. But it can take longer. In the worst case, it can take up to 254 days. However, this is not to be assumed since giving up negative thoughts and replacing them with a thought stop, for example, is not particularly time consuming.

After all, only you can know. Always ask yourself how you're doing with it. Have you already overcome negative thinking? The following procedure has proven to be very successful:

Week one: Use the technique you have chosen consistently. In the end, you ask yourself how you are doing with it and whether you might want to try a different technique. If, yes, stick with this new technique for another week.

Second and third week: Practice the technique, for example the Delete Button. I recommend staying on the ball for three weeks so that the change is pro found enough.

Each additional week: Stay another week with the technique. By the way, you're welcome to change if it motivates you. If you feel that the negative feeling has not yet been completely released or accepted, hang on to it for another week.

In a nutshell

- The 5-step peace process is a step-by-step

guide suitable for all kinds of negative feelings.

- You start by classifying the intensity and frequency of your feelings.
- With the help of the Emotions Matrix you choose suitable techniques.
- Write down, at least for a few days, when your emotions arise and in what situations. This will give you important insights.
- Now apply the techniques. You should do this at least one to three weeks or until your feelings are either gone or you can accept them.
- Be open to additional resources. This is an optional step, but I recommend you do it.

How to practically control the most important emotions - in 5 easy steps

"Spring is when the soul thinks colorful again."
– Anonymous

In this chapter...

- Many examples of how to apply the 5-step peace process in practice
- How to manage your worries and fears
- A special, powerful breathing technique against panic
- The 5-step peace process with unforgiveness
- Special powerful tips against depression
- How to tame the rage monster

Worries, fears, and panic: the most powerful techniques

Fear can have a variety of expressions. It ranges from slight restlessness to panic. There are generalized anxiety disorders or phobias, such as arachnophobia (fear of spiders). All these fear variants are described in this book under the term "fear." Fear is a very unpleasant feeling, so we have a strong tendency to avoid it. As a result, we may become more and more self-constricted as we want to avoid anxious situations.

But let us look at the positive side of fear before we come to the peace process. How is there a positive side to fear? Yes! Every feeling has a signal. Fear tells you that "something negative will happen in the future." So fear gives you a signal that you should take care of yourself or your loved ones. Fear is an indication that you should do something. So if you feel any form of fear, consider whether there might be something to this signal. Do you have an exam, and you are ill-prepared? Or do you have to give a speech and have very little time to practice it? This signal should always be observed.

Now we come to the 5-step peace process against fear:

1. Determine the intensity and frequency: All types of anxiety are unpleasant. So it is quite possible that although your fear only occurs several times a week, you already classify it as "permanent." That is perfectly permissible. The classification into intensity and frequency is all about your subjective perception.

2. Selection of techniques: Here, use the Emotions Matrix; it's the key. A tip: one technique that helps particularly well with anxiety is the 4-7-8 breath.

3. When and what circumstances? Write down here exactly when you have these fears, under which circumstances, and the intensity.

4. The Work: If your feelings are very intense or occur frequently, you have chosen The Work. Consider consulting a therapist if you have very intense fears. Now identify your beliefs. Do The Work regularly for one to three weeks. You'll see your fears get better soon.

Tip: When you do The Work, ask yourself how likely the unpleasant event you are afraid of will occur.

Fred's afraid of losing his job. He had lost his two previous jobs and developed this fear. In fact, there was no danger to him. I advised him to work on his fears with The Work. He had the belief: "I will lose my job. That's terrible." On The Work's first question, Fred could see that he could not know if he would lose his job. That helped him but not completely. I recommended that he assess the likelihood that he would be dismissed. He should fill out the following small form[1]: Fred selected the "3" box. It is important that we fill out this form in writing and not just in our minds. Fred could visually see that the probability was very low. This has given him a lot of relief.

What is the negative event that I predict will happen?				*"I'm gonna lose my job"*					
In reality, how likely is it that this negative event will occur?									
1	2	~~3~~	4	5	6	7	8	9	10
Absolutely unlikely		highly unlikely		approx. 50% probability of occurrence		very likely		almost certain	

---

[1] I have taken this form from the book *Cognitive Behavioural Therapy Workbook For Dummies.*

95

This form can be very helpful for fears. The important thing is that you actually do it in writing. It always has a stronger effect than if you just get it through your head.

5. Additional resources: Breathing techniques are very effective for anxiety. I want you to meet two of them. The first is a breathing technique from yoga. It is very famous, and you can use it for all kinds of anxiety, from mild restlessness to panic.

Alternate Nostril Breathing

Goal: relaxation

Technique:

1. Sit on a chair with your back straight or cross-legged on the floor. You can lie too. Make sure that your head is not raised.

Source: http://www.sarvyoga.com/anulom-vilom-pranayama-steps-and-benefits/

2. Inhale and exhale deeply: Inhale deeply and

slowly. Exhale and let all air out of your lungs. Stay loose and relaxed.

3. Close left nostril: Gently close your left nostril with your ring finger.

4. Breathe in right: Breathe in through your right nostril.

5. Close right: Gently close your right nostril with your thumb.

Source: http://www.sarvyoga.com/anulom-vilom-pranayama-steps-and-benefits/

6. Exhale and inhale left: Exhale and in through your left nostril.

7. Close left: Now gently close your left nostril.

8. Exhale right: Exhale through the right nostril.

9. 10 x: Take at least 10 breaths like this.

How often? How long? Use this breathing any time

you feel stressed or need a little more relaxation.

Tips & Tricks:

- **Effective against anxiety and stress**: Alternate Nostril Breathing is excellent against anxiety and stress, it is very relaxing. Try it out. You will immediately notice a calming effect.
- **Explain video**: Watch the Alternate Nostril Breathing in the following video: https://www.youtube.com/watch?v=8VwufJr Uhic
- **Abdominal Breathing**: You should inhale and exhale into the abdomen all the time.
- **Less than 10x**: You don't always have to take ten breaths. Less works too.

The next technique I would like to introduce to you is a very strong and effective breathing technique that you can use especially in case of **panic**. Of course, you can also use it on lightor fears, but it's like shooting at sparrows with a shotgun. The breathing technique is a combination of two very effective techniques.

On the one hand, the **4-7-8 breath**, which in itself is excellent against anxiety and panic. This i s combined with another technique that works on an energetic level: **Dr. Shioya's Long Life Breath**. This breathing is quite demanding. But with a little practice, you'll master it easily. This means that if you suffer from panic attacks, you should first practice this breathing in quiet moments.

Anti-Panic Breathing

Goal: calming down

Technique:

1. Touch your palate with the tip of your tongue just behind your upper incisors. Keep your tongue in this position throughout your breathing.

2. Exhale completely through your mouth and lips with a "woosh" sound.

3. Close your mouth and inhale silently through your nose, counting to four. Say or think, "I inhale peace and relaxation."

4. Hold your breath, counting to seven. Tighten your anus firmly. Say or think: "I am completely safe and calm."

5. Exhale through your mouth as if under step two, counting to eight. Release the tension in your anus. Say or think, "All fear and negative thoughts leave me."

Repeat steps three, four, and five for a total of four breaths.

How often? How long? Every time panic rises.

Tips & Tricks:

- **This breathing technique is incredibly strong against panic**. The 4-7-8 breath is in itself very good and effective against fears and panic. This has been scientifically proven. This breathing technique here is the reinforced version — the anti-panic turbo, so to speak.

- **In addition to 4-7-8 breath, there are two elements**: 1. you tighten your anus while holding your breath. This is a technique from Kundalini yoga. This is also used for energizing. 2) Suggestions are also used. You can change these, by the way, if you like other suggestions better. One suggestion I found very effective was: "Fear comes and goes." However, you can only use the suggestions when you no longer need to count because you can't count and make suggestions at the same time. So, first practice until you can skip counting and then recite the suggestions.

- **Learn in steps**: If you practice this breathing technique, start to tighten your anus while holding your breath and do so vigorously. If you have internalized this, then add the suggestions during breathing. All this sounds complicated, but it's not. You'll get the hang of it after a few times. And then you will have a technique that will help you in your panic.

- **Baby Feelings**: Try to control the panic as soon as it comes up. As a baby feeling it is easier to control them. When you do the breathing, everything is quickly released.

- **Tip**: Many people affected by panic attacks are afraid that the panic attack will not stop.

That's not true, of course. Panic is an extreme alarm state of the body. This cannot be maintained for long. Don't worry about it; the panic will definitely pass. The panic will even pass without the use of any techniques. It just takes longer.

Fred suffered from panic. In a coaching session, I had shown him the Anti-Panic breathing. "You have to practice it, because if you panic, it's very hard to do anything at all. So you have to have the technique right and be able to do it in your sleep," I warned. "All right, I will," Fred replied. He had one or two panic attacks a week. Two days after the session he had the next one. It caught him immediately after getting up. Fred inhaled for four seconds. In this intense situation, he could not remember the affirmation he had prepared. He held his breath for seven seconds, tightening his sphincter. Then he breathed out for eight seconds through his mouth, like blowing out birthday candles. He omitted the affirmations. After a few breaths the panic subsided. "I was so relieved," he confessed to me in the next session, "for the first time I had the feeling of having my panic under control." "You did a great job," I said. "It doesn't matter that you left out the affirmations -- it worked anyway. Still, train your breathing a little more so that you can do it in your sleep because panic is an extreme situation," I explained. With the help of Anti-Panic breathing, Fred was able to almost dissolve his panic within a few weeks.

So, that's it on the subject of anxiety. If you follow the 5-step process, your fears will quickly get better. As always, it's important that you keep your eye on the ball. Your fears have built up over the years, and unfortunately, they won't go away in a few days. But they're leaving! Maybe you're lucky, and it only takes a week for them to disappear or for you to accept them. But maybe it will take you a little longer, maybe a few weeks or even months. Stay with it! It's worth it!

Unforgiveness: We don't have to knock someone out first to forgive

Each of us has been hurt before. A co-worker bullied us, we were teased at school, our partner cheated on us. Such events can lead to unforgiveness.

Unforgiveness means that we are not at peace with an injury from the past.

We had the example of Sara who couldn't forgive her ex-boyfriend Mark. This was expressed in such a way that she regularly thought about these events and felt feelings of offense and anger. So Sara is not at peace with the past events. Unforgiveness has a high price.

Costs of unforgiveness

Happiness research has shown in many studies that irreconcilability has a similar effect as stress. This means that when our blood pressure and heart rate rise, cortisol and adrenaline are released. Our immune system is weakened, we age faster, and the probability of degenerative diseases such as diabetes and cancer increase. When we think only of our injuries, stress is triggered. In doing so, we only harm ourselves and not the perpetrator. At the same time, many studies have shown that forgiveness has a very positive effect. Those who can forgive more easily are happier and happier with their lives. Polloma and Gallup proved this in a US study. Mothers who were abandoned by their husbands suffered less from anxiety and depression when they had really forgiven them. In a study, Witvliet, Ludwig, and Van der Laan compared people who forgive with those who had not forgiven. They were supposed to imagine the perpetrator who hurt them. People who had not forgiven got a higher heart rate just by the idea, the blood pressure rose, and the skin resistance increased. This was not the case with people who had forgiven their perpetrators. So, scientifically proven, unforgiveness is bad for our health. Instead of quarreling with our past, we should forgive.

"Forgive others not because they deserve forgiveness, but because you deserve peace."

Forgiveness means that we are at peace with the hurtful events of the past.

Three points are important in this context:

- **Forgiveness does not mean that we approve of the act**. A betrayal is a betrayal is a betrayal. Sara forgiving Mark doesn't suddenly turn a cheat into a good deed.
- **Unforgiveness only harms the victim**. Sara feels offense and anger several times a day. It could cause her health problems. Mark, the perpetrator, doesn't even notice. So you forgive to make yourself feel better, not the perpetrator.
- **Forgiveness is purely internal**. Forgiveness means that Sara is at peace with the offending event. It doesn't mean Sara has to be friends with her former best friend again. So forgiveness has nothing to do with external actions but only with inner peace.

Now we come to the work of unforgiveness. We are using the 5-step peace process.

The 5-Step Peace Process for Forgiveness

1. Determine the intensity and frequency: How strong is your unforgiveness? How often do the feelings occur and how intense are they?

For Sara, unforgiving emotions occurred several times a day. So the frequency is "often." The intensity of the feelings fluctuated. Sara said the feelings were sometimes "medium," sometimes even "quite intense." Sometimes it is not easy to estimate the intensity of feelings. That's not bad at all. Then listen to your gut feeling.

2. Choice of techniques: Now choose the technique that suits the intensity of your feelings.

Häufigkeit / Intensität	selten (mehrmals wöchentlich)	gelegentlich (mind. 1 x pro Tag)	oft (mehrmals / häufig pro Tag)	ständig (mehrmals stündlich)
1 = leicht	Expansion	Expansion	Expansion	Expansion
2 = mittel	Defusion/ 4-7-8-Atmung	Defusion/ 4-7-8-Atmung	Defusion/ 4-7-8-Atmung	Defusion/ 4-7-8-Atmung
3 = ziemlich	Sedona/ Löschtaste	Sedona/Löschtaste	Sedona/Löschtaste	TheWork
4 = sehr	Sedona/ Löschtaste	TheWork	TheWork	TheWork

Since Sara was not sure whether the intensity was "medium" or "quite intense," she could choose between four techniques: Defusion, 4-7-8 breath, Sedona method, and the Delete Button. We decided on the following approach: She used the Delete Button exercise for a few days. Then she practiced the Sedona method for a few days. These two techniques were in her favor right from the start. After a week's testing, Sara finally opted for the Sedona method.

With the intensity "medium" and "quite intense," you can choose between two methods. Either you decide according to your gut feeling or you try each of the methods for a few days.

3. When and what circumstances? Enter into an app or notebook exactly when and under what circumstances your irreconcilability occurs.

Sara was amazed to find that her unforgiveness was

stronger and more frequent after visiting her mother. She and her mother had a good relationship and met frequently. Sara had not noticed a connection before. Her mother had divorced her father after he had cheated on her. Sara was reminded of this by her mother's visit. Her own unforgiveness towards her ex-boyfriend became stronger as a result. By recognizing this connection, Sara was able to deal more consciously with the unforgiveness and let it go more easily.

4. The Work: This step is optional. You should only do it if you have chosen an intensity of "very intense."

Sara decided against doing The Work. That was a good decision because the irreconcilability decreased considerably after a short time. However, if the irreconcilability had remained persistent, I would have recommended Sara to use The Work, even if the intensity did not reach "very intense."

5. Additional Resources: There are effective forgiveness exercises. One of them is the Heart Focus. It is a kind of meditation. It brings you inner peace and cultivates positive and peaceful feelings.

Heart Focus[1]

Goal: relaxation, training of positive, peaceful feelings

Technique:

1. Sitting posture: Take a comfortable position in which you can stay for 10 to 15 minutes. Sitting is best. This promotes attention and alertness.

2. Abdominal breathing: Focus your attention on your breath as it flows in and out. When you inhale, allow the air to gently squeeze out your belly. As you exhale, consciously relax your belly so that it feels soft. Do this for about five minutes.

3. Reminder: Remember an experience with another person where you felt a strong feeling of love or imagine a landscape that fills you with wonder and tranquility. Please do not take a person you wish to forgive for this exercise.

4. Intensify memory: Try to make this memory come alive. You can support this by asking yourself what exactly you have seen, heard, felt, and smelled. Put yourself, as far as possible, into this memory and experience the peaceful and loving feelings. You can strengthen this by making the inner picture brighter,

---

[1] The Heart Focus originates from the great book Forgive for Good: A Proven Prescription for Health and Happiness (2010) by Fred Luskin.

the colors stronger and bigger. Often it is pleasant to feel these good feelings in the heart area.

5. Abide in peace: Keep these peaceful feelings as long as possible. Do not put yourself under pressure. If your attention is wandering, direct it to the gentle lifting and lowering of your belly. Then return to step three.

End: After 10-15 minutes slowly open your eyes. Stretch out and return to your daily activities.

How many times? How long? You should practice the Heart Focus technique at least three times a week. Do this for three weeks. The yardstick is what your forgiveness looks like. If you have the impression that after two weeks the unforgiveness is already dissolved, then stop.

Tips & Tricks:

- **Why do we do the heart focus?** We relax with the Heart Focus. At the same time we indulge in pleasant feelings. We train not to be taken in by thoughts. As we practice Heart Focus, thoughts and stories emerge, but we simply return to the breath. In this way we create distance from our thoughts. This is an important ability if we want to forgive. When the old story about our injury reappears, we have now learned not to be taken in by it.
- **Practice on fixed days**: For example, on Sundays, Wednesdays, and Fridays.

- **Practice at fixed times**: This helps to develop a habit. I am a friend of morning routines. That's very practical; we get up and do the Heart Gocus technique without thinking about it. After getting up, our critical mind isn't so active, we don't think so much about whether to do the Heart Focus or not. We simply do it.

Sara was able to greatly diminish her unforgiveness. Since she didn't like The Work so much, I suggested the technique of Heart Focus.

Let's see how Sara practiced the heart focus:

1. Sitting posture: Sara just came home from work and was still tense. She had a comfortable armchair in her living room. She dimmed the light and took a seat for the exercise. Sara set her mobile phone to silent as a precaution.

2. Abdominal breathing: Sara closed her eyes and breathed deeply into and out of her stomach for about five minutes. She was able to relax well, and after five minutes she had shaken off all the tension of work.

3. Memory: Sara imagined a wonderful beach from her last vacation in Thailand. She laid on a couch and looked at the white, fine sandy beach and the sea that stretched far in front of her. Sara relaxed even more.

4. Intensify memory: Sara asked herself what she had seen, felt and heard. She saw the beach and the sea and tried to remember details. She heard the subtle roar of

the sea and the soft voices of other people. She en-
larged the picture and intensified the colors. This al-
lowed her to reawaken the feelings she had on vaca-
tion at that time. She felt very calm and moved at the
same time. This scenery touched her heart. At the same
time, she felt longing.

5. Abide in peace*: Sara held these memories and feel-*
ings for a few minutes. Then her thoughts wavered
away. When she noticed it, she returned to the
memory.

End*: After 15 minutes, Sara slowly opened her eyes.*
She remained seated for a while and stretched.

"It was a very pleasant experience," she reported later.
"I felt well and balanced."

Depression: hardly known antidotes

Depression has become a widespread disease. So if
you have depression, you have a lot of company.
When it comes to depression, it's always worth con-
sidering going to a therapist. But maybe you only
have a depressive mood. Everyone feels highs and
lows in their lives, and that doesn't have to be a depression. But it is good if you get clarity about it.
Therefore look at the following table. If necessary,
you can discuss the completed chart with your therapist. In the table, tick the symptoms you are experi-
encing.

Nr.	Symptoms
1	I always feel sad, empty, down and depressed.
2	I generally have little interest in what's going on around me.
3	My appetite and weight have either increased or decreased a lot.
4	I have trouble sleeping.
5	I'm feeling slow and lacking in motivation.
6	I feel guilty or worthless.
7	It's hard for me to concentrate or make decisions.
8	I feel like it's better if I'm dead.

Source: Cognitive Behavioural Therapy Workbook For Dummies.

If you have checked the first or second symptom and four others and have already done so for at least two weeks, then you are probably depressed. If you're not going to psychotherapy yet, I strongly recommend that you do so. The techniques in this book may not be able to help you.

Costs of depression

Depression affects your life. Depression has its costs. Reflect on the following questions:

- What have you missed in your life due to depression?
- What strategies have you used to deal with depression?
- Do you spend time avoiding unwanted negative thoughts and feelings?
- How effective have the strategies you have used so far against depression been?
- Can you estimate how much time and energy you normally use every day to avoid depres-

sive thoughts and feelings?

Probably the strategies you have used so far to get rid of your depression are not effective. The techniques and strategies in this book will certainly help you.

The 5-Step Process for Depression

Now we get down to business. Enough talk — let's do the 5-step process. I know it's often not easy for a depressed person to get their act together; often, it's difficult to even want to do anything about the depression. Still, I believe in you! Don't hesitate long, just start with the 5-step process. Now! One more thing, depressions are persistent. That's why I recommend that you integrate The Work into your process. So don't skip step four. I also recommend some additional resources that are very effective.

1. Determine the intensity and frequency.

Sabine was a beautiful young woman. She had been suffering from depression for several weeks. She had separated from her boyfriend, and her studies did not give her any pleasure. It was a constant subliminal condition. She didn't feel like doing anything, and when her friends called her or sent her a message, she didn't feel like doing anything. She barely left her apartment. She classified the intensity as "medium." The frequency with "constantly."

2. Selection of the techniques

Frequency ⟍ Intensity	rare (several times a week)	occasionally (at least 1 x per day)	often (several times/frequently per day)	permanent (several times per hour)
1 = light	Expansion	Expansion	Expansion	Expansion
2 = moderate	Defusion/ 4-7-8 Breath	Defusion/ 4-7-8 Breath	Defusion/ 4-7-8 Breath	Defusion/ 4-7-8 Breath
3 = quite	Sedona/ Delete Button	Sedona/ Delete Button	Sedona/ Delete Button	TheWork
4 = very	Sedona/ Delete Button	TheWork	TheWork	TheWork

Sabine selected The Work in addition to the Delete Button.

3. When and what circumstances?

Here Sabine found out that her depressions were stronger in the morning than in the evening. So we agreed that she would meet a friend in the morning to do some sports. In the "Additional Resources" section, you will see that exercise is a great remedy for depression.

4. The Work

Sabine did The Work every evening. That made it easier for her schedule. She was surprised at the abstruse thoughts she sometimes had. "My God," she said to me. "I am so unfriendly and hard on myself. Why do I do that?" I told her about my talkative Darth Vader in my head. "That's normal," I replied. "the voices in our heads are usually not friendly."

5. Additional resources

For depression there are some great resources that can help you:

1 Exercise! There are thousands of studies that have proven the positive health effects of exercise. It's less known that exercise also has positive effects on our mood. A basic study was conducted by Stanford University: The participants were divided into three groups. The first group received antidepressants. The second group did exercise; the participants rode their bikes for 40 minutes three times a week. The third group did both. This means that they took antidepressants and did exercise. The result was interesting: After four months, the result was the same in all three groups! There were no differences. In 60% of the participants there was a clear improvement. This means that exercise works just as well as medicine. The study was continued, and it was observed how many of the 60% relapsed. In other words, their depression worsened again. After ten months, the results were astonishing: The group who had taken antidepressants had a relapse rate of 38%. In the group with drugs and exercise there was a relapse rate of 31%. And now, hold on: The group that only did exercise had a relapse rate of 9%, believe it or not! This means that exercise was clearly superior to medication in terms of long-term effects.

Amazing, isn't it? And it is not a lot of sport! 40 minutes of cycling or jogging three times a week is sufficient. Try it out!

2. Three Good Things Technique: Three Good Things has proven to be a very successful intervention: depressions diminish, and happiness increases. Even up to six months later, after the participants of a study applied this positive daily review, the positive effects were still measurable.[1] Even in severely depressed subjects, some of whom were unable to get out of bed, this technique was surprisingly effective. After only two weeks, 94% improved significantly.[2]

Three Good Things

Goal: training to savor the good things

Technique: The technique Three Good Things is about finding three events and writing them down. You can deepen the experiences by asking "why?" in each case. In Three Good Things there are three alternative variants: "Pleasant experiences," "Use your strengths," and "Meaningful experiences."

Choose one of these variants:

First variation: pleasant experiences. Ask yourself: "What was pleasant today? Or ask yourself: "What

---

[1] Seligman / Stehen / Park / Peterson (2005): "Positive Psychology Progress: Empirical Validation of Interventions", American Psychologist, 60(5), 410–421.
[2] Seligman (2011): Authentic Happiness: Using the New Positive Psychology to Realise Your Potential for Lasting Fulfilment.

was beautiful today?" Find three pleasant experiences. Of course you can write more at any time, but three things are enough. You can deepen the experience by asking afterwards: "Why was that pleasant?" Here are a few examples.

Question: "What was beautiful today?" Answer: "I played with my little son this morning." Question: "Why?" Answer: "It was so sweet to cuddle with him. He laughed so much, and his sweet eyes...."

Question: "What was pleasant today?" Answer: "I rode my bike today. That was fun." Question: "Why?" Answer: "Actually I wanted to watch a TV series. But I got my act together after all. It was nice because it was a good feeling to move. I also rode through a beautiful forest, which was really good."

The "why question" deepens the experience. You can answer the "why" question completely freely -- you can't do anything wrong.

Second variation: use your strengths. Here you reflect on three occasions today in which you have used your strengths. Ask yourself: "Where have I used my strengths today?" You can deepen this by asking the question "Why?" afterwards. Here are a few examples.

Question: "Where have I used my strengths today?" Answer: "I played with my little son this morning." Question: "Why?" Answer: "I'm a loving father and able to play well with the little one."

Question: "Where have I put my strengths today?"
Answer: "I rode my bike today. It was fun." Question:
"Why?" Answer: "I'm disciplined, and although I was
tired, I still rode a bike."

Third variation: meaningful experiences. At the
end of the day you write down three meaningful experiences you had today. Ask yourself the question:
"What was meaningful today?" and then: "Why?"
Here are a few examples.

Question: "What was meaningful today? Answer: "I
played with my little son this morning." Question:
"Why?" Answer: "My son gives meaning to my life."

Question: "What was meaningful today?" Answer:
"Today the sunset was so beautiful." Question:
"Why?" Answer: "It was a meaningful experience because it showed me how beautiful the world is and
that there is more than everyday life."

How many times? How long? The positive daily review is done daily in the evening, in writing. You can
use it as long as it is right for you.

Tips & Tricks:

- **What is the easiest thing for you to do?**
  Happiness research follows the motto
  "Strengthen strengths and manage weakness-
  es." This means that you should choose the
  variant that is easiest for you. Personally, I like
  the "strength variant" of the positive daily re-

view best. I like the "meaningfulness variant" least of all. What suits you best? You can vary at any time. That is, tonight you do the "Strength Day Review," tomorrow the "Pleasant Day Review."

- **Use a journal**: It has been shown that it is best to do the daily review in writing. If you just think about it, then it's easier for your thoughts to digress. Suddenly you find yourself thinking about today's work and where something has gone wrong. That's why it's stronger when you do it in writing. I have published *The 90-Day Happiness Journal*. It is a great and easy way to become happier (click on the image!):

- **Energizing breathing technique:** You know what? Sometimes you are dog-tired, but you still have to be in top shape at a meeting. Or you might need a nap, but your sweet, and sometimes exhausting, children want to be supervised. There are many examples where we just don't have time to recharge our batteries. Wouldn't it be nice if we had a technique that gives us an energy boost in seconds and without any side effects? And yes, there really is such a technique. I call it breath espresso. It's a breathing technique that quickly gives us energy — without any side effects.

Breath espresso

Goal: energy boost

Technique:

1. Preparation: Breathe in and out three times deep into the abdomen.

2. Breathe out suddenly from the nose: You do this by quickly pressing your upper abdomen inwards and pushing out the air. The main participants are the upper abdominal muscles. They are pressed strongly and abruptly inwards. The exhalation lasts only about one second.

3. Passive inhalation: Just let go, and the air will be sucked in automatically. Inhalation is also short, one to two seconds at a time.

4. Breathe out again from the nose abruptly and in passively: Take 10 breaths in this way and then breathe normally again.

Do you feel energized now?

Tips & Tricks:

- **Explanation video:** Under this link, I explain the breath espresso in a video: http://detlefbeeker.de/energie-schub-auf-knopfdruck-der-atem-espresso/
- **Without preparation:** After some practice, you can skip the preparation.
- **Less is possible:** You don't always have to take 10 breaths. Less is possible. The main thing is that you feel comfortable and the situation allows it.
- **Increase up to 100:** You can gradually increase the number of breaths. Up to 100 breaths are possible. Don't hurry with it. Until you reach the 100 breaths, you can take weeks and even months. It is important that you feel comfortable. Always pay attention to yourself and your body.
- **In the morning after getting up:** To build up energy for the day, you can do the breathing espresso for two minutes immediately after getting up.
- **Do not do this before sleeping:** The breath espresso is stimulating. Do not do it before going to bed.
- **Caution:** If you experience pain or dizziness,

stop the exercise and sit still for a long time, breathing calmly and deeply.

- **Contraindications:** Breath espresso should not be used by patients with heart disease, high blood pressure, dizziness, epilepsy, stroke, hernia, stomach ulcer, colitis, pulmonary emphysema, after surgery, or during menstruation or pregnancy.
- **Tip:** You can increase the effect even more by tapping the middle of your breastbone with four fingertips. This stimulates the thymus gland.

I really want to recommend these additional resources to you. Especially the first two work very well. I know there is a lot of material and a lot to do. So don't overwhelm yourself. But practice at least one of the three suggested resources.

Anger and rage: the exact instructions and two unknown weapons

Anger is part of the human experience. In itself, it is nothing negative or bad. Anger becomes a problem when we express it aggressively or even violently. Anger and rage arise when we feel attacked, threatened, insulted, or unfairly treated.

Anger and rage happen. In some cultures more, in others less. You may also be familiar with the stereotypical argument of an Italian couple. The woman throws plates, and the man screams. Two minutes later, they lie in each other's arms and kiss. The German culture of conflict is calmer.

Look at the following table and fill it out. This will give you a better feeling as to whether your anger and rage are a problem or not.

In the last 6 months, if I got angry...	Never	Once	More than once
I got depressed			
I had a fight			
I destroyed something			
I fought with loved ones			
I hurt myself			
I said terrible things to others			
I endangered professional matters			
I got in trouble with the police			
I drove riskily			
I felt ashamed and guilty			

If you come to the conclusion that you want to fight your anger, this is the right place for you. I will introduce you to a step-by-step solution to get your anger under control.

As with all feelings, the easiest way to get anger under control is when it's still a baby feeling. By that I mean that this anger has just arisen. The anger is hard to stop when a stress response has been triggered. If your system feels threatened, then a stress reaction is triggered, i.e. you flee or you fight.

This is a relic from times long past when we still had to be afraid of being attacked by a tiger. If a threat was perceived, then our rational thinking was switched off, and we were prepared lightning fast for fleeing or fighting.

In today's time this is not optimal. If we quarrel with our partner, and he attacks us verbally, it is not life-threatening. We do not have to flee or fight. But unfortunately, our rational thinking is switched off, and our amygdala gains the upper hand. The amygdala is a small part of the brain that is responsible for the stress reaction. In other words, we lose control. Have you ever experienced this? Suddenly your anger is so strong that you say or do things you wouldn't otherwise do. In retrospect you wonder how something like that could happen. Here the amygdala was in play. That means we have to try not to trigger that stress reaction in the first place.

Lara was very popular. She considered herself to be an uncomplicated person. But if you asked her boyfriend, Brando, he was of a completely different opinion: "She quickly gets angry! When she is angry, she is another person. She has thrown her mobile phone at me more than once. Fortunately it never hit me. She just broke my headset the other day." Apart from these intense fights, they had a good relationship. Nevertheless, the fights put a lot of strain on the partnership. Several times they almost broke up because of these fights. That's why it was important for Lara to get her anger and the fights under control.

5-step peace process

1. Determine the intensity and frequency: How strong is your anger or rage? How often do the feelings occur, and how intense are they?

Lara found her own anger to be very strong, so the intensity was four. The two fought about once or twice a week. Actually Lara should have selected "rarely" here. Since her subjective feeling was that this was still too frequent, she indicated "occasionally."

2. Choice of techniques: Now choose the technique that suits your intensity.

Frequency / Intensity	rare (several times a week)	occasionally (at least 1 x per day)	often (several times/frequently per day)	permanent (several times per hour)
1 = light	Expansion	Expansion	Expansion	Expansion
2 = moderate	Defusion/ 4-7-8 Breath	Defusion/ 4-7-8 Breath	Defusion/ 4-7-8 Breath	Defusion/ 4-7-8 Breath
3 = quite	Sedona/ Delete Button	Sedona/ Delete Button	Sedona/ Delete Button	TheWork
4 = very	Sedona/ Delete Button	TheWork	TheWork	TheWork

Using the table, Lara chose The Work. The second technique she used was the Sedona method and 4-7-8 breath. She decided to try them both for a few days and then commit herself.

3. When and what circumstances? Enter into an app or notebook exactly when and under what circumstances your anger or rage occurs.

Lara found out that she got angry faster after having a long work day. So stress in other areas of her life encouraged her to get angry.

4. The Work: This step is optional. You should only do it if you have chosen an intensity of "very strong."

She filled out the worksheet to the rage-triggering situations. Through this she discovered her beliefs and negative thoughts. It was not easy for Lara to deal with these beliefs. Often anger and hurt came up again. Lara continued consistently and bravely. She decoded her beliefs, such as: " Brando never listens to me! He does not love me! He loved his ex-girlfriend much more than he loved me. He doesn't care about my feelings! When I confront him, he dodges or looks at his stupid notebook."

Lara did The Work daily for three weeks. Therefore, every evening she took up her beliefs and edited them with The Work. The Work is a powerful method and often works from the very first application. With Lara it took a little longer. But already after one week she could feel that her anger and rage were diminishing. In acute situations, both techniques, Sedona and 4-7-8 breath, helped very well. So she simply kept both, and decided on a case-by-case basis. Today Lara has her anger under control. Her relationship is better than ever.

5. Additional resources:

I'd like to introduce two more techniques from Mark

Goulston's ingenious book How to Deal with the Irrational and Impossible People in Your Life. The book is about how we deal with difficult and irrational people. A very important factor is that we remain calm in conflict situations. In the book, several weapons are presented which are very effective. Two of these "weapons" that I will introduce to you are strong anti-anger techniques.

Weapon #1: Interpret an attack as an opportunity

Anger and rage always have something to do with other people. For example, we argue with our boss, our neighbor, or our partner. Anger arises when we feel attacked.

Lara fought with her boyfriend Brando. She accused him of not listening to her. He countered back with irritation: "Don't annoy me! I'm working on my notebook right now! Don't always take yourself so seriously!" That was an attack. Normally Lara would have shot back. This time she used Weapon #1.

What is meant by seeing an attack as an opportunity? Our normal reaction is to respond to an attack with a counterattack. But we can also choose to see such an attack as a way to stay calm and relaxed. There is a nice Buddhist story on this subject:

Once a father came to Buddha very upset. His son wanted to become a disciple of Buddha and travel with him. His father was afraid of losing his son. He blamed Buddha. He became angry and filled with rage and in-

sulted the Buddha. He attacked him and even became loud. Buddha listened to him. He remained calm. When the father had finished, Buddha said, "I understand you, but it is your anger and not mine." Then, according to legend, the father threw himself at the feed of Buddha and immediately became his disciple.

A beautiful story. Wouldn't it be cool if we could stay as calm as Buddha? Why do we have to make our peace dependent on other people? When others are angry with us, it very often has nothing to do with us. So why should we get upset? Well, that's the enlightened perspective. We normal people get upset quickly when we are attacked. But that doesn't mean that we can't try to develop further.

" Don't let other people's behavior disturb your inner peace."
— Dalai Lama

This is the background of Weapon #1. We see this attack as an opportunity to evolve. In the face of the storm, we remain calm. We do not let our peace be taken away.

How do we do this practically? Take the sentence

"Chance for Serenity"

as an affirmation in the argument. Say this affirmation to yourself again and again until you have actually become more relaxed. If this is the case, you can direct the argument into constructive channels. Perhaps you can say: "I don't like the way you personally attack me. Nevertheless, I want to understand exactly what is important to you. Could you say it again in a calm tone?"

Weapon #2: Visualize your mentors

It's not easy to stay calm when you want to get angry. Your mentors can help you with that. What do I mean by mentors? These are teachers and role models in your life. For example, I like Byron Katie very much. She is very calm and peaceful. You can also take a fictitious mentor. Maybe a character from a film like Neo from the film Matrix or Gandalf from The Lord of the Rings Trilogy. But it can also be your mother or your father, an old friend or another relative.

Visualization of your mentors

Goal: to alleviate anger and rage

Technique:

1. Short break: If you feel your anger surge, ask your mentors for help. Take a short break for this. For example, you can tell your "opponent" that you have to go to the toilet for a short time.

2. Visualize your mentors now: Imagine how their serenity and love fills you. Imagine what advice they give you. Feel how your anger is weakening and inner peace is giving way.

3. Thank your mentors: Return now to the discussion.

4. **How often? How long?** Every time you feel anger rise.

Tips & Tricks:

- **Other situations**: You can also ask your mentors for help in other situations. If you have fears, a difficult conversation, etc.
- **Play around with the visualization**: You can imagine the mentors hovering above your head and shining bright light and energy into you. Another picture would be when you visualize a mentor in the middle of your chest. There he radiates bright light and energy that fills your whole body. See which image feels best for you.

Sara also tried this technique. She chose Jesus and Wonder Woman as mentors. Sara had seen the movie "Wonder Woman" in the cinema and was impressed by the strength and kindness. During the next fight with her partner, she breathed in and out deeply into her stomach. Then she visualized Jesus and Wonder Woman floating cross-legged above her head. Both were surrounded by light. She imagined Jesus looking at her kindly and saying, "Let go of your anger. You love him; you should not hurt him." Now she imagined how both mentors let their energy flow into her. This technique calmed Sara down quickly. She thanked her mentors.

That's it on the subject of anger and rage. I wish you good luck getting these emotions under control.

In a nutshell

- You can use the 5-step peace process for all negative emotions.
- For fears and panic, I recommend two extremely calming breathing techniques as additional resources.
- Unforgiveness makes you sick. The technique Heart Focus is a powerful tool to release unforgiveness.
- Depression is surprisingly widespread. Please consider if you would like to visit a therapist. As additional resources for depression, exercise is especially effective. But also the positive daily review and the breath espresso are very powerful.
- Anger and rage can destroy many a relationship. Once anger is there, the rational mind is switched off. As additional resources, I recommend two anti-rage weapons.

Summary

"If it costs your inner peace, it's too expensive."
– Anonymous

In the following table, all the techniques of this book are summarized again. From the table you can see what techniques are suitable for each emotional intensity. Some techniques, such as 4-7-8 breath, are intended for acute situations. This means that if, for example, fear is present, you can use 4-7-8 breath. Some techniques are preventive, such as The Work. You will then find "yes" in the column accordingly. The table also contains the techniques of the "additional resources." Under "Hints" you can see to which emotions the respective technique currently refers.

One more thing. Sometimes you get your emotions under control quickly. Sometimes, however, it takes longer. If you've been struggling with fears for years, they won't disappear within a few days. Please have some patience. Success will surely come. Endurance is the number one success factor. If you consistently follow the 5-step peace process, you will be able to free yourself from your unwanted feelings.

	intensity	acute	prophylactic	emotion
Expansion	light	Yes		
4-7-8 Breath	moderate	Yes		
Defusion	moderate	Yes		
Sedona-Method	quite	Yes	yes	
Delete Button	quite	yes		
TheWork	very		Yes	
Alternate nostril breath	quite/very	Yes		Anxieties
Anti Panic-breath	very	Yes		Panic
Heart Fokus	moderate		Yes	Unforgiveness
Sport	moderate/quite		Yes	Depression
3 good things	moderate/quite		Yes	Depression
Breath Espresso	moderate/quite	Yes		Depression
Weapon #1	quite/very	Yes		Anger
Weapon #2	quite/very	Yes		Anger

Free Gift

*"The clearest sign of wisdom is a
consistently good mood."*
— Michel de Montaigne

As a thank you, I would like to give you a gift: the
book **18 Surprising Good-Mood Tips** (52 pages). You can download it at the following link:

http://detlefbeeker.de/en/gift/

Do you remember the first time you fell in love? Was
not everything suddenly nice? How wonderful the
blue sky looked, with its white clouds. Even the rain
you could enjoy. What if you could have this lovely
mood all the time?

In this book, you will learn:

- Body parts to press to relieve stress and
  improve your mood and health.

- Proven mental tactics that will put you in a good mood in seconds.
- Secret Yoga techniques that will easily increase your good mood.
- Which unknown piece of music is scientifically proven to be the best stress reducer?
- What you can learn from James Bond and how it gives you relaxation and self-confidence.
- How you can relax in 10 seconds.
- Practice this fantastic technique and get fresh and revitalized.
- Which apps are the best to relieve your stress and give you relaxation and serenity?
- The latest trend: The Fidget Cube and how it works.
- Bonus: The new generation of good mood techniques
- ...and much more.

Download this book NOW for **free,** so that you'll be guaranteed more joy, serenity, and happiness with the help of the best techniques.

http://detlefbeeker.de/en/gift/

You belong to extraordinary 3.2%

"Not the beginning is rewarded, but only the perseverance."

Do you hear the applause? This is from the author! You deserve it. Why? Because only 10% of readers go beyond the first chapter of a book, and you've even read the whole book! So you bring things to an end - an important skill! Also, you are among the special group of readers who read self-help books. Only 32% of readers do so. By the way, we have something in common. I love self-help books too! Together, we belong to selected 3.2%. Well, if that is not worth the applause!

I put a lot of passion into this book. That's why I'm glad that you found it so interesting to read. It gives me the courage to ask you for a small favor. It costs you nothing, but it would help me enormously: **Would you take a minute or two and write a quick review?** Two or three short sentences are enough. You can write them on the book page.

Maybe it seems unimportant, but every single review counts. Your positive review helps me continue to work as an independent author and write books that help people.

Thank you so much!

Warm regards,

Detlef Beeker

Website of the author: http://detlefbeeker.de/en/

PS: If you do not like the book, please let me know. Any kind of feedback is valuable to me. Just write me an email to detlef@detlefbeeker.de.

To the series
"5 minutes daily for a better life."

"Success is the sum of small efforts, repeated day in and day out." — R. Collier

This quote is the philosophy of this series. We don't have to do much. Small actions can be enough. However, we should note the following:

- We must apply them in the long term. We need perseverance.
- We should choose our actions wisely. This is what the Pareto principle tells us:

Pareto principle: 20% of the effort leads to 80% of the result. This is an empirical law, which was discovered by Vilfredo Pareto. For example, 80% of a company's revenue is generated by 20% of its customers.

Isn't that great? We have to choose the means we use cleverly. So we can achieve 80% of the desired result with little effort. We can then come up with a winning formula:

Success = skillful, small actions + persistence

This formula is the basis of the series "5 Minutes Daily for a Better Life." And yes, it is possible. Change doesn't always have to be time-consuming. Science used to think that you have to exercise for at least three hours a week to promote good health. Today we know that 30 minutes a week is enough if you train skillfully. That's not even five minutes a day.

contents of all linked pages which were changed after the link was set up. For illegal, incorrect or incomplete contents and especially for damages resulting from the use or non-use of such information, only the provider of the page to which reference was made is liable, but not the author of this book.

Detlef Beeker

Printed in Great Britain
by Amazon